Love Your Food Again

Ingredient Substitutions for Allergy-Free Living

SUSAN J. HARDESTY

Hardesty, Susan J.
Love your food again: ingredient substitutions for allergy-free living / Susan J. Hardesty.
ISBN: 1508555419
ISBN-13: 978-1508555414

Edited by Allison M. Sidhu

DEDICATION

This book is dedicated to everyone who struggles daily with figuring out what to eat due to food allergies, weight, or the ever-so-popular leaky gut and autoimmune diseases.

The average person does not realize the daily struggle that people with health issues endure as they seek out ingredient substitutions for recipes, or food replacements in general. Nor do they understand the trauma dining out or attending social gatherings can cause, when everything centers around food. Generally, there is nothing you can eat unless you B.Y.O.S or M. (Bring Your Own Snack or Meal).

I know that pain and frustration so well. My hope is that this book will give *you* a bit of hope for your future meal preparations—because cooking and eating should be fun!

With a little practice, you will be able to dazzle your family and friends with your creative and tasty recipes. This book is about learning to creatively use other foods for substitutions in recipes, and I include a few recipes of my own as examples. My hope is that you will use the information in this book and begin to experiment, creating your own dishes that will fulfill your family's dietary needs.

CONTENTS

ACKNOWLEDGMENTS

I would first and foremost like to thank the staff at the Institute for Integrative Nutrition for planting the seed and guiding me along the way as I wrote this book.

I would especially like to thank my ever-so-patient editor, Allison M. Sidhu, for her knowledge and guidance in the correction and revision process, along with her great attention to detail. She has been my right arm.

Special thanks to my fiancé Jeff, who put up with my many hours spent in front of the computer day after day, and in the kitchen working out my recipe flops and successes. Special thanks also go to Jeff's son Nathan, my taste-tester, who boldly sampled and critiqued the recipes that I created, made with out-of-the-ordinary ingredients at times. I am truly grateful for your support.

1) MY JOURNEY

For as long as I can remember, I have spent my life suffering the wrath of multiple food allergies. As a child, I knew something wasn't right, but I never associated what I ate with my symptoms because they would not appear right away. It might be an hour later, a few hours, or even the next day before I would have any symptoms. I thought everyone had issues with gas and a bloated tummy.

When I was in grade school, there were even a few times when my eyes would almost swell shut and my top lip would swell. I actually have a picture of myself holding my little sister one Christmas while I was having a flare-up. Mom just thought I was allergic to our cat. Little did we know, the reaction was actually related to the foods I had eaten.

Like most kids, I used to love sitting on the couch and consuming large quantities of C. C. Bigs or Oreos, dunking them in my glass of milk. Or there were the many trips to the Valley Bell Dairy for a hot fudge sundae or a milkshake, not realizing hours later or possibly the next day that the sneezing, congestion, bloated tummy and tight chest that I experienced were all reactions to the foods I had eaten and enjoyed so much.

The first step I took in the quest to figure out what was going on with my allergies was when I was nineteen. I went to visit an ear, nose and throat allergy specialist who did a RAST blood test. The doctor told me the results showed many allergens, so he would have to test even further with allergy skin prick testing. The results came back with a list of so many allergy-inducing foods that it made my head spin! Thus began the journey of eliminating some of these foods, of which many were my favorites, and getting weekly allergy injections.

This was a painful and expensive process. After a while I decided to discontinue the shots and try to control my allergies the best I could on my own by staying away from problem foods. I thought I was doing a great job eliminating these foods, but I was still experiencing many of the same symptoms—sneezing, bloating and constipation, brain fog, and lethargy. I blamed this on all of the antihistamines I had been consuming. So, I set out once again to try to gain answers and relief.

As I got older, other health issues started to crop up. Back in the 1980's, there wasn't a lot of information available about what are known today as autoimmune diseases. I heard about this thing called "gluten," and wondered if it was something that might be affecting me. Although I was not tested for a gluten allergy, I felt it could be the culprit based on my symptoms—feeling bloated, gassy, and like I had a heavy stomach after eating breads, pastas, cakes, crackers, and even cookies.

In January of 2010, I went on a 21-day detox/cleanse program where I only ate vegetables and drank protein shakes, before slowly introducing meat back into my diet after eleven days. The detox really made a difference in how I felt, but with a trip to Hawaii coming up in February, I went back to my old eating habits. I wanted to enjoy myself on vacation, and felt being limited in my food choices would prevent this, except for the severe allergies to dairy, nuts and chocolate that I couldn't ignore.

While I was in Hawaii, the bloating, gas and heaviness in my gut returned. After I returned home, I made the decision to go gluten free. After a few weeks, for the most part, my symptoms were gone. It was at this point that I began learning about gluten-free flours and ingredient substitutions. I also learned that in order to be tested for celiac disease, an autoimmune disease related to the inability to digest wheat gluten, I would have to consume it again or else the levels in my blood would not give accurate test results. The testing itself can only detect celiac disease, but blood testing is not accurate enough yet to test for a gluten allergy or intolerance. The idea of going back to a diet that included gluten and potentially suffering again from the symptoms it caused me was not something I was interested in doing, so I just continued on a gluten-free diet. I am still gluten free to this day.

As a result of testing that I had done in 2015, I have been diagnosed with issues related to digesting carbohydrates, so I am on a grain-free diet. This will not be life-long, but it is necessary until my gut heals and my immune system becomes stronger. Fortunately, I am able to tolerate coconut flour. Since coconuts are from the Arecaceae or palm family, they are considered a fruit, not a nut or a grain. For many people, including myself, coconuts are not a common allergen. This fruit serves as an amazing life-changing substitute for many because it is so versatile. Coconut can be shaved or ground into flour, or made into milk, yogurt, butter and even oil. The water inside the coconut can also be consumed, and the sap collected from coconut flowers can be used for making sugar.

It has been a long journey, one that I am still traveling—not alone, but with the help of a nutritionist, medical testing, supplements and a functional medical doctor. A functional medical doctor looks at the body as a whole, and aims to determine the root cause of a problem rather than just treating the symptoms. This type of doctor spends a great deal of time asking questions pertaining to any symptoms, lifestyle, medical issues from the past, what medicines were taken in the past, sleep patterns, and even family health history. I have also learned the importance of living a healthy lifestyle complete with a whole foods diet and healing herbs, and the positive effect these practices can have on my immune system and organs.

Foodie websites and blogs have been a godsend, guiding me through ingredient substitutions and explaining why some substitutions work while others do not. For example, I have learned about the versatility of cauliflower and how it can be used to make gravy by boiling it until soft, then creaming it in the blender. It can also be a great substitute for rice (See Cauliflower Rice, p. 65). I've also learned, although ground flax meal makes a great egg substitute in baked goods, it is not a good substitute when using coconut flour in a recipe where many eggs are needed. (See Ch. 4, p. 19).

The recipes in this book are nut free, soy free, gluten free and dairy free, but many are not egg free. I do give suggestions for egg substitutions, but please remember if you are baking with coconut flour that it takes a tremendous amount of eggs and can be difficult to use a replacement. I like to use coconut oil for my baking or frying, but you may use butter or oil depending on your food allergy restrictions and personal preferences.

My hope is that this book will serve as a reference guide, to help ease the frustrations encountered when attempting to cook using substitutions, and to give anyone with dietary restrictions ideas that they may be able to incorporate into their own recipes.

2) FOOD ALLERGIES & THE DIET MAZE

Though expert opinion varies when it comes to determining the most prevalent food allergens in today's world, the American Academy of Allergy Asthma & Immunology (AAAAI) is a respected resource that I trust. According to the AAAAI, the most common food allergens are cow's milk, eggs, peanuts, wheat, soy, fish, shellfish and tree nuts.[1] Within some food groups, individuals can also have cross-reactivity to members of the same food family. For example, in the milk family, people may also have an allergic response to ice cream, cheese, and other dairy products, though some people are able to tolerate yogurt or milk from goats. Many people have allergic reactions to foods even after they are cooked. Research in a study conducted by Mount Sinai School of Medicine showed some children can tolerate milk that has been extensively heated in baked foods such as muffins, waffles and cookies. This is because the high temperatures used in baking cause the proteins in milk to break down, thereby reducing the allergic sensitivity of certain individuals to the milk in the product.[2]

Every individual is different, and some people experience allergies to less common foods due to their unique immune response. For example, I have to be careful not to consume too many raw cruciferous vegetables like broccoli and cauliflower, or vegetables in the nightshade family such as tomatoes and peppers, due to the presence of chemical compounds in these vegetables that aggravate my hypothyroidism. I have also learned through other people who have suffered with thyroid issues that the thyroid is not a big fan of sorghum or garbanzo bean flour. Much of this intolerance stems from the autoimmune disorder known as leaky gut syndrome.[3]

Your gut is the foundation of your health. Each time you eat, your gut is responsible for taking in nutrients and keeping out foreign substances. It is possible for your gut to become too permeable, or "leaky." When this happens, things like parasites, bacteria and undigested food enter your bloodstream and challenge your immune system, causing inflammation.[4] It is now known that seventy percent of your immune system is located in your digestive tract, also known as your gut.[5]

Diet Theories

Before getting too excited about one particular diet, know that following the food regime for any particular diet theory may not actually work for you, especially if you suffer from an autoimmune disorder. There is no shortcut to great health and lifestyle. Each creator of a diet theory feels their diet is the best and they will attract many followers who believe this to be true simply because it works for them.

You will find the study of nutritional science is always evolving. Nutritionists disagree greatly about which food groups are most important for the body and what the public should consume to stay healthy. Keep in mind the saying, "one man's food is another man's poison." For every food that you enjoy eating, another person out there experiences adverse digestive or allergic reactions to that same food, and will be unable to consume it. I have researched various diets over the years, trying to figure out the best one to follow based on the foods my body would not have a negative reaction to. I was repeatedly disappointed to discover that my particular food sensitivities did not fit into the boundaries of any specific diet theory. Some of the diet theories I looked at, in the hope that they would help keep me on course towards staying healthy, are listed below.

The Mediterranean diet, for example, is a diet rich in omega-3 fatty acids and low in saturated fats, found to lower rates of heart disease, cancer, and diabetes. This diet consists of natural, whole foods such as whole unprocessed grains, fresh seasonal vegetables and fruits, meat, fish, nuts, dairy, and the abundant use of extra virgin olive oil. This diet excludes other oils, as well as processed and refined foods. The consumption of coffee, wine and meat are highly encouraged, in moderation. Important lifestyle factors include the value placed on relationships, pleasure, leisure, and physical activity, which are all said to help reduce stress and contribute to physical and mental wellbeing.

This diet sounded good and made me think eating and cooking might become fun again, but once I took into consideration my sensitivities to nuts, coffee, wine, dairy, most grains and some meats, I was only left with fruits, vegetables and minimal meat consumption. I decided that even though this is probably a great diet for many others, it is not a diet I could follow.

I took a look at the Atkins diet. This diet is based on high protein and low carbohydrate intake and is set up in four phases. The first phase significantly restricts carbs, focusing on high protein instead. The second phase adds nuts and berries with some dairy, slowly adding more carbs back into the diet. The third phase adds fruit and legumes. The last phase, considered the "lifetime maintenance phase," reintroduces bread and grains. Once adherents to this diet reach the level where they are happy with their weight and the way they feel, they adjust the carbs to an amount that enables them to maintain that level of health.

The main focus of the Atkins diet is burning fat for weight loss. Since I am not looking to lose weight, and considering my food sensitivities and my need for carbohydrates, I would not be able to properly adhere to the various phases of this diet. This was especially true since I do not normally consume a large amount of meat. I decided this was not the diet for me either.

I also gave consideration to a vegetarian diet, which offers varying levels of flexibility. I love fruits and vegetables, so that was a step in the right direction. Vegetarian diets generally exclude meats and fish. Some individuals who follow this diet are considered lacto-ovo vegetarians because they still consume dairy and eggs, whereas an extremely restrictive vegetarian who consumes no meat, fish or dairy and shuns all animal byproducts including honey and leather is known considered a vegan. Veganism entails a strictly plant-based diet.

A vegetarian diet, when properly implemented, is rich in fruits, vegetables, nuts, seeds, legumes and whole grains. As a result, this type of diet is often low in fat and cholesterol, which can decrease the risk of heart disease and diabetes, and aids in combating other obesity-related diseases such as high blood pressure and high cholesterol. Since vegetarians do not consume meat, it is important that they find other sources of protein such as nuts, beans, or grains like buckwheat and quinoa (actually a seed).

This sounded great to me because I enjoy a plant-based diet. That is, until I once again took into consideration my sensitivities to nuts, legumes and grains. Leaving out these crucial elements of a vegetarian diet, which provide adequate protein as well as a variety of vitamins, brings me right back to the inherent importance of meat in my diet in order to stay healthy.

I considered the paleo diet next, also referred to as the primal diet. This diet includes foods that scientists and some doctors believe our caveman ancestors would have consumed before the era of agriculture and the advent of cultivated grains, legumes and processed convenience foods. Packaged foods are full of additives and preservatives to increase shelf life, but they can be harmful to the body.

The paleo diet also includes frequent vigorous exercise and high levels of sun exposure for the production of vitamin D. The sun is a great source of vitamin D, which the body uses to absorb calcium, aiding the strength and formation of bones. This diet includes healthy fats such as coconut oil, olive oil, ghee and avocado oil (See Ch. 4, p. 19).

The paleo diet also includes consumption of organic grass-fed meats including organ meats, organic eggs, seeds and nuts, vegetables, and limited consumption of fruits. Added sugars (meaning those that do not occur naturally, such as the fructose in fruit) are allowed, but may only be consumed in their natural state. For example, raw honey, agave, molasses, and coconut sugar may be consumed as part of the paleo diet. Grains are not allowed. Although quinoa is a seed and not a grain, it is not accepted in the paleo diet and can be difficult for some people to digest, due to its high carbohydrate content.[6] Flour may be consumed if it is produced from almonds or coconuts, since these are grain free.

I consider this style of eating to be very versatile. Although the paleo diet includes nuts, it is the closest that I have come to finding a well-known dietary pattern that meshes with my food sensitivities. Although I do not use almond flour because of my allergy to nuts, I find baking with coconut flour does not seem to affect me in a negative way. Coconuts are botanically considered a fruit rather than a nut, but the FDA considers it a tree nut and as such, some food labeling might say "contains nuts" when referring to coconut or coconut products.

With over one hundred diet theories on record and more being created every day, I have barely scratched the surface.[7] By touching on just a few, I'm able to further illustrate the idea that what works for one person, or even a large group of people, will not work for everyone. It's all about finding what works for you. I am not here to debate which diet theory is the best, but I encourage you to include whole foods and a rainbow of fruits and vegetables in your diet for their vitamins, minerals and fiber. Your body assimilates nutrients from natural, whole food sources easier than anything available in supplement form. This is important in order for the body to heal and function properly.

3) THE SUBSTITUTION MYSTERY

What is Gluten?

Gluten is a protein found in wheat, rye, barley, spelt and kamut. Rice flour and other rice-based products that are described as glutinous do not contain gluten. Rather, this refers to the stickiness or glue-like consistency of the rice when cooked. With the changes that have occurred in agriculture over the years to make some grains more drought- and bug-resistant, the gluten protein has become more difficult for many people to digest, especially if they have compromised immune systems.

There is much debate as to whether oats should be added to the list of gluten-containing grains, since some people are sensitive to a different protein in oats known as avenin.[8] In addition, many companies process oats on the same machinery where grains containing gluten were processed. This means they have been contaminated with the gluten left behind on the equipment, from the minute gluten-containing product dust that was not cleaned before changing over to process a different grain. For celiacs, all of whom are extremely sensitive to gluten, this could be a serious situation, further damaging the villi in their intestines and causing severe digestive, immune and allergic reactions.

If you are unwilling to give up your oats, it is best to purchase them from a reputable company that certifies their oats were grown and processed in a gluten-free facility. According to the United States Food and Drug Administration's (FDA) ruling for foods to be labeled gluten free, products must contain less than 20 parts per million (ppm) of gluten.[9]

Some food companies go even further with testing for gluten to earn the seal of approval from independent organizations that cater to the needs of celiacs. Three organizations, the Gluten Intolerance Group's Gluten-Free Certification Organization (GFCO), the Celiac Sprue Association (CSA), and the National Foundation for Celiac Awareness (NFCA), currently certify products and companies as gluten-free. The GFCO and NFCA require products to contain no more than 10 ppm of gluten, while the CSA requires less than 5 ppm for their seal of approval.[10,11]

The role of gluten in a recipe is to make baked goods such as breads and cakes light and airy, and to give chewiness to baked goods like cookies. It is also used as a binding agent to help other ingredients in the recipe stick together, because it is great at retaining moisture.

The lack of gluten in gluten-free baked goods and other products can affect texture as well as taste. Gluten is used in many processed foods such as gravies, soups and soy sauce as a stabilizer or thickening agent. It can even be found in meats like bacon and lunchmeat. It is important to become a good detective in label reading to protect yourself from unwittingly being "glutenized." An innocent-sounding ingredient like "malt" is a gluten product in disguise. Sometimes an ingredient is just labeled "modified food starch" and does not tell you if it is made from corn, wheat, or another product. If the ingredient on the label is wheat germ, wheat starch, or wheat flour, the product contains gluten.[12]

One of the biggest shocks to consumers with gluten issues is to find out that many health and beauty products and medications also contain gluten. The skin is one of the largest organs of the body and, aside from its ability to be an elimination channel, it can also absorb products into the body. Yes ladies, lipstick products can also contain gluten, which you ingest when you lick or bite your lips. It is best to read labels or contact the manufacturers directly to find out if the products you use or are considering purchasing contain gluten.

The Effects of Gluten

Gluten affects people in various ways and in different scopes of severity within the immune system. There are many adverse symptoms that people suffer from the effects of ingesting gluten, to varying degrees. Keep in mind, not everyone with gluten issues will suffer from all of the same symptoms. Some people feel they do not have symptoms, but internally their gut is being damaged. This can eventually become exacerbated with other symptoms as we get older, or can be brought on by stress or other immune issues such as hypothyroidism or hyperthyroidism.

A short list of symptoms includes but is not limited to constipation, diarrhea, gas, bloating, abdominal pain, skin rashes, hair loss, brain fog (where you feel like you are floating in a dream or have a lack of concentration), muscle aches, depression and anxiety, weight loss or weight gain. I've had many of these. Research has stated a possible connection between gluten intolerance and Alzheimer's disease, as well as a connection with autism.[13,14]

For people with celiac disease, gluten exposure causes damage to the villi inside a person's intestines. Villi are small fingerlike tissues that help with the digestion and absorption of nutrients from food. They also help to move food along through the intestinal tract. After years of gluten exposure, damaged villi in people with celiac disease can be worn down smooth. This causes the food to move too quickly through the intestines, leaving the body before it can be broken down properly, and restricting the chances of adequate nutrient and mineral absorption. This can cause malnourishment and could potentially lead to other bodily dysfunctions and disease.

I have barely begun to touch on gluten and the effects it can have on your immune system. I encourage you to read more about the subject to understand the differences between gluten intolerance and celiac disease.

People who make the choice to become gluten free don't always realize that gluten-free baked goods can be just as calorie dense as baked goods made with gluten-containing flours. This can lead to weight gain, since many flour blends contain starch-based flours as well as sweeteners. Moderation is important, especially for people who have difficulty maintaining a healthy weight.[15,16]

If you feel you might have a problem with gluten, it is best to consult with your health care professional who can do testing, or start you out by doing a 30-day elimination of gluten-containing products and foods from your diet. Pay attention to how your body feels during this time by journaling the foods you are eating and the symptoms you are experiencing, if any. Discuss these with your health care professional, who will work with you to decide if and when to gradually reintroduce gluten back into your diet, then note how you are feeling after eating it again.

Just a few words of caution—if you decide to be tested for gluten intolerance or celiac disease by a medical professional, consumption of the protein must be current in order for it to be detected. In other words, do not start an elimination diet on your own if you plan to get tested. If I went for testing now to find out the severity of the gluten response in my immune system, it is quite possible the results would be negative since I have been eating a gluten-free diet for several years. Based on my own observations, I would not consider consuming gluten again just to have testing done, in light of the pain and the severely negative toll that I believe it took on my body.

Gluten-Free Flour

There are many gluten-free flours to choose from. Knowing their characteristics and how they perform in recipes is important for a wonderfully textured outcome. Bloggers are a great resource, describing what they have found to work best when dealing with various flours. Beth Hillson's article "Power Flours," published in the October/November 2011 issue of *Gluten Free & More* magazine, offers great information on the various flavors and properties of a variety of gluten-free flours.[17]

Hillson discusses seven protein-rich "power flours", which provide more protein than other flours, as well as a host of vitamins and nutrients. They're also higher in fiber, which helps to reduce cholesterol levels. The baked goods from these flours have the ability to make you feel full longer.

The seven flours Hillson discusses are amaranth, buckwheat, flaxseed, chickpea, quinoa, sorghum, and millet. Amaranth flour has a mild nutty taste, milled from the seeds of the tropical amaranth plant. Buckwheat flour, which is not wheat at all, but rather a fruit from the rhubarb family, has a nutty-earthy flavor. Flaxseed meal, or flax meal, made from ground flax seeds, also has a nutty taste. When combined with water, it makes a good egg substitute. Chickpea flour, milled from garbanzo beans, also has a nutty flavor. I use this in my protein flour blend. Quinoa flour, milled from a small grain-like seed native to South America, sports a light, nutty taste that's similar to wild rice. Sorghum flour, milled from the sorghum plant, has a light, sweet taste and is darker in color than most other flours. Millet flour is made from an ancient grain and is grown and consumed worldwide. It is nutrient rich and has a mildly sweet, nut-like flavor.

It is best when baking with these flours to blend them, using no more than thirty percent of each to avoid a heavy, dense texture in your baked goods. Neutral flours like brown rice, white rice and corn are more interchangeable in their ability to blend with each other; however, these are not protein-rich flours like the power flours mentioned earlier.

Power flours should be stored in airtight glass containers and all gluten-free flours should be refrigerated. This is particularly true for power flours with higher fat and protein content, such as amaranth flour and flaxseed meal, which spoil quickly at room temperature. Allow refrigerated flours to return to room temperature before you use them, unless the recipe states otherwise.

It is best when first starting out to find a recipe that was written to be gluten free, instead of trying to convert a regular wheat- and gluten-containing recipe to be gluten free. It will also be less stressful on the baker, which is a big step towards the goal of making one's own gluten-free foods rather than relying on less healthy processed items. I am a testament to the fact—a happy baker is a frequent baker! Many gluten-free flour blends can be used cup for cup in a recipe just like all-purpose flour, to take the guesswork out of baking.

Baking with gluten-free recipes tends to require additional ingredients to keep baked goods from being too dense and crumbly. This also helps them to rise. These ingredients include eggs, xanthan gum, gluten-free baking powder, cornstarch, potato starch, arrowroot powder, and tapioca starch.

My favorite flour when I first became gluten free was brown rice flour. It is so simple to work with. Then I learned about protein-rich flours and the many nutritional benefits they contain. I make my own flour blend with 1 cup each of brown rice, chickpea and sorghum flours. You'll notice in my Punkin' Chunkin' Cookie Bars recipe (p. 82) that this is the blend I use. Lately, my go-to flour is coconut. Although it requires extra moisture, I love anything coconut flavored and the nutritional value it offers. Coconut and almond flours are both used in the paleo diet.

Almond flour is very nutritious and does not have a significant impact on blood sugar like other flours do. This is because it is not a grain-based flour that is rich in carbohydrates. It is high in protein instead. Unlike other alternatives to wheat flour, baked items made with almond flour are said to be moist and delicious. Because of my allergy to nuts, I have not personally baked with this flour or tasted it, but fellow bakers rave about its great taste and ease of use.

Coconut flour, although nutritious, has a bad rap for sucking moisture out of a recipe, so wet ingredients will need to be added to make up for this (i.e. applesauce or eggs). My personal favorite is adding extra pumpkin puree if you don't mind the flavor. You will notice recipes that call for coconut flour will generally be mixed with another type of flour that is considered a starch, except for paleo recipes, which tend to use more eggs instead.[18]

Coconut flour is high in protein, fiber and healthy fat, which can be very filling. When I make my Coconut Pumpkin/Apple Spice Waffles (p. 72), I stay full for many hours. On the nutritious side, coconut flour contains lauric acid, a healthy source of fat, and is also a good source of manganese, choline, biotin, vitamin C and thiamin.

Baking with coconut flour does have its challenges, which include some of the following: It is difficult to substitute coconut flour on a 1:1 ratio in place of wheat flour, due to the moisture-absorbing properties of coconut flour. Most recipes require 1/4-1/3 cup of coconut flour for every cup of grain-based flour. Extra liquid ingredients such as eggs would then need to be added to compensate for the moisture-absorbing power of the coconut flour. Add six beaten eggs to one cup of coconut flour, plus one cup of additional liquid such as your choice of milk or milk substitute.

Since coconut flour tends to be dry and clumpy, it is best to sift the flour before adding to a recipe. Sifting is also helpful if you're using it for coating when frying meat or vegetables. This can be done in the same way that you might use regular flour or breadcrumbs.

There have been many recipe flops along the way on my gluten-free journey. Until you gain knowledge and experience as to which flours and ingredients work well together, it is wise not to skimp or change a recipe.

When I read a recipe on someone's blog, I learn so much from readers' comments. We are so fortunate to have the internet today for exchanging knowledge, as compared to when our parents and grandparents first made their recipes.

Because there are no preservatives in flours or home-baked goodies like there are in processed store-bought foods, flours and yummy-licious baked masterpieces have a short shelf life. That is, if they last long enough to worry about storing before they are gobbled up! I have learned from experience that placing baked items in the fridge tends to dry them out quickly, unless it is something like bread that will be toasted. I always freeze extra cookies and sweet breads that I have made in lidded containers or freezer bags. I have even been known to eat these treats straight out of the freezer without letting them thaw out first.

The Rise and Fall of Baked Goods

Baking soda is also known as sodium bicarbonate. When baking soda is combined with an acidic ingredient like honey, lemon juice, cream of tartar, apple cider vinegar, or buttermilk, this results in a chemical reaction that produces bubbles, starting the process immediately when mixed with the moist ingredients. This process produces carbon dioxide that expands with heat, giving rise to baked goods.

Baking powder on the other hand is also made from sodium bicarbonate, with the addition of an acidic agent known as cream of tartar and a starch. Cream of tartar, or potassium bitartrate, is a common household chemical used in baking. It is a byproduct of the winemaking process that is created when grapes are fermented. Like baking soda, it produces a gas when it comes in contact with liquid ingredients, but most of the process is completed once heat is applied in the baking process. Cream of tartar acts as a stabilizer, and is also added when making whipped cream or whipped egg whites.

So how do you know when to use baking soda and when to use baking powder? Baking soda needs to be combined with an acidic ingredient to be used successfully in a recipe. As I mentioned before, these include honey, lemon juice, cream of tartar, apple cider vinegar, and buttermilk. This will help your baked goods to rise. Baking soda can cause your final product to have a bitter taste if an acidic ingredient is not added to the recipe. It cannot go through the complete chemical reaction process, which could prevent your baked item from rising properly. Since baking powder already contains an acidic ingredient (cream of tartar), it does not necessitate the addition of an acidic ingredient to do its job properly.

You can use baking powder in place of baking soda by using three times the baking powder that a recipe calls for. For example, to replace 1 teaspoon of baking soda, you will need 3 teaspoons of baking powder. On the other hand, substituting straight baking soda for baking powder could cause your recipe to flop. If you don't have baking powder on hand, you can always make your own using the following substitutions:[19]

1 teaspoon baking powder= ¼ teaspoon baking soda +
½ teaspoon apple cider vinegar, cream of tartar, or lemon juice

4) THE SUBSTITUTION CONNECTION

Got Dairy-Free Milk?

For those of you with a dairy allergy, vegetarians, or those who just plain want to eliminate milk from your diet, you have lots of options. Some substitutions that can be used in recipes are rice milk, soymilk, coconut milk (canned and boxed), hemp milk, flax milk and goat's milk. Generally the ratio is a 1:1 replacement. Special treats like pudding, ice cream or whipped topping should be approached with caution when using substitutions for regular milk, as they may not have the same properties that make the treat set up nicely. This is because cow's milk is thicker, due to its fat content. To make up for this, you may need to decrease the quantity of milk substitute just a little and increase the amount of starch or thickening agent in these types of dishes.

Most milk substitutes do not have the same acid content as regular milk. This may affect your recipe, especially in the case of baked goods, unless you add baking soda or baking powder. This choice of course depends on whether other ingredients in the recipe are adequately acidic. As was mentioned in Ch. 3 (p. 11), these are leavening agents that help the recipe to rise.

Be cautious when purchasing canned and boxed milk, as some of these products may contain additives like guar gum or carrageenan, which are used as stabilizers. These may cause allergic reactions in some people, especially those with autoimmune disorders and leaky gut syndrome. It is so important to be a good label detective.

Coconut milk in a can is richer than coconut milk in a box. Placing the can in the refrigerator will cause the cream to separate and rise to the top, leaving the coconut milk in the bottom portion of the can. The solid portion at the top of the can is referred to as coconut cream. It can be used in many recipes where a rich cream base is called for. Keep in mind, canned coconut milk has a strong coconut flavor that will shine through, depending on what other ingredients are used in the recipe. Canned coconut cream can also be used to make Coconut Whipped Topping (p. 87) or icing for a Devil's Food Coconut Cake (p. 88). For best results, place the can in the refrigerator overnight. I even like to put my mixing bowl and beaters in the fridge so everything is cold when I'm ready to cook. Once the topping or frosting has been made, it should be kept in the refrigerator, as well as any goodies that have been iced.

Both canned and boxed coconut milk are available in sweetened and unsweetened varieties. I prefer to buy unsweetened coconut milk to have on hand for a variety of uses. When a recipe calls for the sweetened variety, I just add honey in small amounts, tasting along the way until my sweet tooth is satisfied.

Making coconut milk from scratch is ridiculously easy! Just add 1 cup of organic unsweetened coconut flakes to 1 cup of water. If more is needed for your recipe, just double amount of coconut and water. Bring just to a boil, then turn off the heat and let it sit until cooled. Pour into a blender and blend for approximately 5 minutes. Strain the coconut flakes out (use a fine mesh strainer or cheesecloth) and there you have it: coconut milk. To sweeten the milk, just add honey to suit your sweet tooth.

The milk will become solid on top when you refrigerate it—this is the fat rising to the surface. It can easily be blended back in if you let the milk return to room temperature and shake or stir. If you're in a hurry, this can be accomplished more quickly by heating the milk slightly on the stove while stirring. I like to reuse the strained coconut by drying it out on paper towels, then freezing it for later use when I want to make a recipe that calls for coconut. The flavor is not as intense, but it still works well in baked goods, breakfast porridges and granola.

A Note on Sweetening Eats & Treats

There are a number of natural sugar alternatives available that will help you to avoid the use of artificial sweeteners. I avoid artificial sweeteners because of the toxic effects they can have on the body. I know of a family member and a friend who both were diagnosed with debilitating health issues (intestinal issues, muscle aches and pains) that their doctors linked back to the large amount of artificial sweeteners they consumed. Their paths to recovery have been long, but their symptoms seem to be subsiding.

Agave Nectar is made from a desert plant and is sometimes used as a sweetener in baked goods and pancakes, mixed with fruit, and added to other foods where sugar or honey would normally be used. Agave nectar is extremely sweet. If you are using it in a recipe to replace sugar, the amount should be reduced by ¼ of the total sugar called for. In addition, since agave nectar is a liquid, other liquids in the recipe should be reduced by ¼ if used in baking. Even though agave has a low glycemic index, experts have stated it is okay for diabetic consumption; however, there is a counter-argument that claims it contains more fructose than corn syrup.[20]

Coconut Sugar, also called coconut palm sugar, is caramel in color and looks similar to regular brown sugar. Sap collected from the flowering coconut buds is boiled down and dehydrated into sugar. The quality of coconut sugar is affected by the age of the trees, weather conditions for that season, and processing. Coconut sugar contains various micronutrients including amino acids, potassium, magnesium and iron. This type of sugar is great for many different baking and cooking uses, it tastes like brown sugar and is often said to have a high mineral content, but it is also expensive. It is important to make sure you purchase pure coconut sugar, not a product that has been mixed with other sugars.

Coconut sugar is caramel in color and looks similar to regular brown sugar, except it has a low glycemic index. This means it doesn't raise blood sugar like regular sugars do, so it has been touted as being a good sugar for diabetics. Remember to be cautious, as some diabetics are affected differently by various types of sugar products as well as differences in brands. Keep in mind if you are watching calories- the calorie content is similar to granulated sugar.

If you choose to use coconut sugar in a recipe that calls for regular granulated sugar, substitute in equal amounts. I have even used it in place of brown sugar. Coconut sugar can be purchased in health food stores and online, as well as in some grocery and bulk food stores.[21]

Stevia is actually an herb. The leaves have been used for many years to sweeten tea and coffee. Stevia has recently gained widespread popularity and is now grown around the world. Although these statements have not been approved by the FDA, experts claim stevia does not affect blood sugar levels like granulated sugar does. This means it is a better option for diabetics to use, as well as people who are suffering from candida.[22]

Stevia is one hundred percent natural and up to three hundred times sweeter than granulated sugar. Raw natural stevia is available in leaf form, dried and sold whole or ground. It tends to be pricey. Stevia used for cooking is generally processed into a white powder, with fillers such as lactose and maltodextrin added to tone down the bitter aftertaste. There are many brands on the market, so it is important to read the label to make sure any added fillers are not on your allergen list. It can also be purchased in liquid form. Because my family uses a lot of stevia, I am going to grow it in my garden this year. I checked with a local nursery and they should have stevia plants coming in for the new growing season (yea!)

Using stevia as a substitute in cooking can be good for some items but not for others. It is difficult to use when making candies and caramels because stevia does not melt like granulated sugar, but it works for cookies and other baked goods. In general, the sweetness level can vary depending on the brand. Stevia can also have a bitter aftertaste unless you use a brand high in steviosides (the natural extract from the stevia leaf). Pure stevioside is a white or slightly off-white color. Products with a stevioside content below ninety percent generally have a tan or yellowish color.[23]

Here is a general guide for you to use when replacing sugar with stevia. Keep in mind- adjustments may need to be made based on the brand of stevia used, and the amount of sweetness preferred. Because many brands of stevia contain fillers, it may be wise to check the box or the company's website for their own conversion measurements.[24]

1 cup sugar = 1 teaspoon stevia powder or liquid concentrate

1 tablespoon sugar = ¼ teaspoon stevia powder or 6-9 drops liquid concentrate

1 teaspoon sugar = 1/16 teaspoon of stevia powder or 2-4 drops liquid concentrate

Blackstrap Molasses is the byproduct of refining white sugar, produced after boiling down sugar cane three times. Blackstrap has the most nutritional benefit in comparison to other grades of molasses. It is a good source of iron, calcium, copper, manganese, potassium and magnesium. Experts claim blackstrap molasses can be easier on diabetics, since the blood sugar in the body remains stabilized after use.[25]

In my experience, blackstrap molasses can be a little overpowering. It adds a somewhat earthy flavor to dishes that contain pumpkin or ginger, including many holiday recipes. I like to add a small amount to my morning groats or baked beans.

When substituting blackstrap molasses for granulated sugar, use 1-1/3 cups molasses to replace every cup of granulated sugar, and reduce the amount of liquid in the recipe by 5 tablespoons. Molasses is more acidic than sugar, so you should also add ½ teaspoon baking soda for each cup of blackstrap used. Again, replace no more than half the granulated sugar called for in a recipe with blackstrap molasses or you will have a strong, yet less sweet flavor that you may not be happy with. In recipes that call for a liquid sweetener like honey or maple syrup, I generally substitute with a combination of half honey and half blackstrap molasses.[26]

Recipes that I have made using molasses tend to darken a lot quicker than those that use granulated sugar or some other type of sweetener. It is often best to reduce the oven temperature by 25 degrees when baking cookies or quick breads. This may increase the cooking time, but it is easier to check on the item during the baking process and increase the baking time than to be disappointed like I was with a dish that's too dark, dried out on top but wet in the middle.

Raw Honey is the most nutritious form of honey. It contains 18 amino acids, vitamins and minerals, as well as trace amounts of probiotics. Most honey sold in grocery stores is processed and pasteurized, and may contain additives. Processing also eliminates the nutritional value of raw honey. Some brands, when you read the ingredients, actually contain little to no natural honey and are mostly comprised of fillers. It is best to purchase honey from a health food store or directly from a beekeeper, if you can. I just ordered two more gallons from a local beekeeper and it was less expensive than what I would have paid for one gallon at the nearest health food store.

Honey will keep for a long, long time. If it starts to crystallize, adding a little heat will help bring it back to liquid form. Honey is one of my favorite go-to granulated sugar substitutes to use in recipes and it can be tolerated by many diabetics.

To substitute for granulated sugar, use ¾ cup plus 1 tablespoon honey in place of 1 cup sugar, and reduce the other liquid ingredients by 2 tablespoons. Unless the recipe includes sour cream or buttermilk, add a pinch of baking soda to neutralize the acidity.

Maple Syrup is a natural sweetener made from the sap of maple trees. It is low in calories and high in nutrient value with a lower glycemic index than granulated sugar. When purchasing maple syrup, it is important to buy pure, unprocessed syrup with no additives. During the summer I like to purchase maple syrup from a local farmer who sells his product at our farmers' market.

In baking, replace granulated sugar with the same amount of maple syrup, and reduce the amount of liquid by about half a cup. Because maple syrup can be pretty expensive, I often use half maple syrup and half honey in recipes.[27]

The Skinny on Cooking With Fats and Oils

There is much debate surrounding cooking fats and oils and the effect they may have on the body. Our bodies need the right kind of fats and oils in order to function properly. This helps with mineral absorption and helps fat-soluble vitamins to make their way through the body. Many medical experts believe oils derived from plants, such as corn, safflower, canola, peanut and soybean oil, are perfectly healthy. The problem with this theory is that these oils have often been extracted using high heat and highly refined processes to prolong their shelf life. This creates dangerous free radicals, leading to chronic inflammation throughout the body that has been linked to autoimmune diseases and cancer. An example of a healthy element that is often removed during processing is conjugated linoleic acid (CLA), a naturally-occurring healthy trans fat that is chemically removed to inhibit spoilage. Vitamin E is another example, as it is neutralized or destroyed by high temperatures and pressure.[28]

Margarine and shortening are made by taking room temperature liquid oils like soy, corn or canola and mixing them with tiny metal particles, which are then exposed to hydrogen gas at high temperatures and pressure. Emulsifiers and starch are added to the mixture to give it better consistency. To remove unpleasant odors, the oil is subjected again to high temperatures, with dyes and flavorings added to make the product resemble butter, before it is poured and molded into containers. This process is known as *hydrogenation*, and it causes a restructuring of the atoms and molecules on the fatty acid chain, yielding a *trans* formation or *trans fats*. These types of fats are unrecognized by the digestive system and stored in the fat cells of the body, blocking the utilization of essential fatty acids and potentially causing increased blood cholesterol, inflammation, and other immune system dysfunctions.[29]

Out With the Trans Fats and in With Poly-Unsaturated Fats?

The government's health experts have told us in recent years to replace trans fats with polyunsaturated vegetable oils like soybean oil. In response, many fast food restaurants have eagerly jumped on board and now that's what they cook your fries in. And hey, aren't these foods and oils supposed to be good for us, since they contain essential fatty acids (EFAs)? EFAs (omega-3s and omega-6s) are important for the function and production of our cellular membranes, protecting us from viruses, bacteria and allergens, and playing an important role in the prevention of autoimmune diseases. They are the primary healing agents in our bodies, but because our bodies can't produce them, we must get them in adequate quantities from our diet instead.[30]

When it comes to processed foods, oils and EFAs, omega-3s are so sensitive to light and oxygen that many manufacturers have removed them to promote a longer shelf life for their products. Omega-6s are found in high quantities in plant oils derived from corn, safflower, peanuts and soybeans. The omega-6 content of canola oil is not quite as high as the aforementioned oils, but it is still not a good cooking oil because of its high sulfur content and the ease with which it becomes rancid. Baked goods made with canola oil tend to develop mold very quickly. Also, during the deodorizing process, the omega-3s found in processed canola oil are transformed into trans fatty acids, similar to what's found in margarine. Despite this fact, it is still used widely.[31]

With Americans' high rate of consumption of processed foods and oils, paired with a low intake of whole foods, our healthy 1:1 omega-6 to omega-3 ratio has become out of balance. This has contributed to our many societal health problems, including heart disease, depressed immune function, and cancer. We are now getting our omega-3s from highly refined vegetable oils, as well as grain-fattened meats. Feeding grain instead of grass to livestock creates large amounts of omega-6s in the meat and fat, as opposed to grass-fed meat where the omega-6 to omega-3 ratios remain more in balance.[32]

Cooking With Good Fats and Oils

Coconut Oil is a great choice for high-heat cooking due to its high smoke point. This oil is liquid at room temperatures above 75 degrees, but solid when stored in the fridge or in colder climates. Keep coconut oil out of direct sunlight and it will last for years without going rancid.

Even though coconut oil does not contain omega-3s or omega-6s, because it is a saturated fat rather than a polyunsaturated fat, it offers many health benefits. It is high in lauric acid, a fatty acid with strong antifungal and antimicrobial properties. Coconut oil also contains fatty acids called medium chain triglycerides (MCTs). MCTs make their way quickly to the liver during the digestive process, providing a great source of energy.

Many people (myself included) use coconut oil for baking, frying and general cooking. I even add it to my hot tea. Coconut and coconut oil are consumed extensively by people living in tropical climates where there are not as many health problems as there are today in the United States. I can't say enough positive things about coconut oil and coconut-containing foods.

Olive Oil contains a high percentage of oleic acid, a natural fatty acid that occurs in some plants and animals. This is an omega-9 fatty acid and is considered a healthy source of fat that's rich in antioxidants. This makes olive oil ideal for low-heat cooking or for use in uncooked items like salad dressings, dips, or my Zucchini Ribbon Salad (p. 63). It is touted for its heart-healthy benefits and is very popular in Italian restaurants and the Mediterranean diet.

Although coconut oil is better than olive oil for extreme high-heat cooking, olive oil can still be used at moderate temperatures. It is best to store olive oil in a cool, dry, dark cabinet to keep it from going rancid. Hands down, this is my second favorite oil to cook with.

Ghee is preferred by many people for use in frying and high-heat cooking for its very intense, buttery flavor. It is important to make sure your ghee is made from organic unsalted butter sourced from grass-fed cows. This ensures that it will contain high amounts of omega-3 fatty acids, and it will be free from any potentially harmful chemicals and excess water that are often used in commercially-processed butter.

Ghee and clarified butter are very similar, so similar that many misinformed people believe they are one and the same (I was one of them). They can both be used for cooking, but they have a few differences. Clarified butter is cooked just to the point where water evaporates and the milk solids separate and sink. Ghee is cooked a little longer until the milk solids caramelize, and has a very fragrant buttery smell.

Some people who cannot tolerate butter are able to eat ghee and clarified butter without any problems. This is because the milk fats and solids have been removed during the cooking process, including the lactose (which many people have trouble digesting) and leaving only the butterfat.[33]

Cooking with Animal Fats is preferred by many. I can remember many meals at my grandmother's house when I was younger where she always had a can full of bacon grease sitting on the stove. She would use it for cooking just about everything and she never refrigerated it! Back in my grandmother's day, modern concerns about commercial feedlots, hormones and steroid use were not as prevalent as they are today. As time progressed, the medical world jumped in, proclaiming the harmful effects these fats and oils can have on cholesterol and heart health. Many studies have shown this is not the underlying culprit of disease and related health issues, although countless people still believe it to be true.[34]

The popularity of animal fats has come back around again with people using lard, bacon grease (see my Pepper Bacon Mashed Tater Cakes, p. 61), duck fat and other animal fats to cook with. These sources give added flavoring to dishes. The best quality animal-based fats come from organic grass-fed animals instead of those that are fed grain. It is important to know the source of your meat in order to be sure that the animals were not given hormones and harmful antibiotics, which remain in the meat and fat after it has been processed. Purchasing meats from local farmers and health food stores should provide the necessary contact information to further investigate how the animals were raised and processed.

Other Oil Replacements

Some people like to use unsweetened applesauce, pumpkin puree, or a fruit puree as a substitute in baking instead of oil, as this reduces some of the fat and calories. Use an even 1:1 substitute. Also keep in mind, using fruit instead of fat may add a little more sweetness and flavor, depending on which type of puree is used.

Can you say Eggless?

Eggs are so common in our everyday recipes and baked goods, but many people with dietary intolerances, certain preferences, or allergies scratch their heads trying to figure out a suitable substitute for this incredibly multifunctional ingredient.

Eggs have three main functions in cooking and baking: they add moisture, they bind ingredients together, and they leaven. It is important to know what function the egg is performing in your recipe.

- If the egg is the main liquid ingredient, it adds moisture.
- If the recipe contains an egg and baking powder or baking soda, or if there are no other components in the recipe that would be able to hold the other ingredients together (like breadcrumbs, nuts, or flour), the egg is the binder.
- If there are no other rising agents, the egg is the leavening.

If replacing NO more than 1 or 2 eggs in a recipe, the following ingredients can be used as substitutes. Keep in mind- this could change the texture of your baked goods.[35,36]

Finding the right egg substitute for your baked goods is a matter of preference as well as trial and error. Although I have not found a good replacement for whipped egg whites, there are several egg replacements that may be used in baked goods. Just keep the egg's function in the recipe in mind when choosing replacements.

Arrowroot is a starch from the rootstock of a tropical plant that is ground to a fine white powder. It is used as a thickening agent in foods. Arrowroot thickens at a lower temperature than flour and does not mix well with milk. It should be mixed with a cool liquid before adding to a hot liquid or food and should only be heated until a mixture thickens, since overheating will cause it to break down and begin thinning. Substitute one teaspoon of arrowroot powder plus one teaspoon of water for one egg. You may need to add additional liquid to the recipe.

Guar Gum is a powder that is ground from guar beans, native to Asia. Guar gum is economical because it has almost eight times the water-thickening consistency of cornstarch, and only a small quantity is needed in most recipes. It is best used in cold foods such as ice cream or pudding, and mixed with milk substitutes such as coconut milk or rice milk. It can also be used in baked goods but not in foods that have a high acid content (such as those containing lemon juice) since the acid can cause the guar gum to lose its thickening ability. The amount used will vary depending on the baked good. When baking cakes, use ¾ teaspoon guar gum per cup of flour. For muffins and quick breads, add 1 teaspoon guar gum per cup of flour. For yeast breads, add 1-½ to 2 teaspoons guar gum per cup of flour.[37]

Xanthan Gum is produced by a microorganism called *Xanthomonas campestris*, which is fed a diet of corn, wheat or soy sugar. This sounds gross, but it really isn't. It is important to know the source of the sugar if you have allergies to corn or soy.[38] Fortunately, gluten-free varieties are available. Xanthan gum is used as a thickening agent in baked goods, salad dressings and sauces. Mix 1/4 teaspoon xanthan gum with 1/4 cup of water to replace one egg, and let the mixture stand until it thickens before incorporating into a recipe. If replacing more than one egg, xanthan gum may not be the best substitute as it may cause baked goods to be heavy or slimy with an unpleasant aftertaste.[39]

Psyllium Husk Powder can be purchased at your local health food store and via many online sites. Add 1-2 tablespoons to your wet ingredients and let the mixture soak for no more than 2 minutes because it tends to dry out fast. Although your recipe will seem dry, psyllium retains water much like chia seeds do and it works well as a binder.

Flax Meal is made from ground flax seeds, which are high in omega-3s. The seeds must be ground into meal in order to make them more absorbent, to make their nutrients more bioavailable, and to make them easier to digest. Flax meal can be used as a partial flour substitute or also as a binding agent in place of eggs. For every egg, combine 1 tablespoon of flax meal with 3 tablespoons of warm water. Stir and let sit for 5-10 minutes to thicken before combining with other ingredients. Flax meal has become very popular in recent years. It can be purchased at most groceries, health food stores, and even online.

Chia Seeds come from a flowering plant in the mint family that is native to Mexico. The use of chia seeds in baking is quite common. They are often sprinkled into flour mixes to add a nutritional boost to cakes and cookies. Chia seeds do not have to be ground like flax seeds, but they are also rich in omega-3 fatty acids. With the recent rise in popularity of chia seeds, they are readily available at groceries, health food stores and online.

Chia seeds are great binding agents due to their highly soluble fiber, and they are also considered hydrophilic or water absorbing. They can absorb up to 12 times their own weight in water, forming a gel-like substance that locks in moisture, thus improving the overall structure of breads, pastries and cakes. Just like flax meal, to replace an egg mix 1 tablespoon of chia seeds with 3 tablespoons of warm water and set aside to thicken for approximately 5-10 minutes.

Gelatin Powder is a colorless protein made from the collagen found in animal parts. As stomach-turning as this sounds, it actually contains amino acids and aids in digestion. Gelatin powder can be purchased at supermarkets in the baking section, but it is best to purchase organic gelatin to free you from any worries about it coming from animals that have been given growth hormones or antibiotics. Health food stores as well as online sources are your best bets for finding organic gelatin. To replace one egg, combine 1 tablespoon of unflavored gelatin powder with 3 tablespoons of cold water, and set aside for approximately 5-10 minutes until it turns the consistency of applesauce. Stir in 2 tablespoons plus 1 teaspoon of boiling water. Add immediately to the rest of your ingredients or the gelatin will solidify and will need to be reheated.

Silken Tofu is made from soymilk. Unlike regular tofu which is boiled, curdled and pressed in a manner similar to dairy-based cheese, silken tofu is coagulated without curdling the milk. It is not pressed, so it has higher water content than regular tofu. The creamy texture of silken tofu is ideal for use in puddings, desserts and as an egg replacement. It can be used in recipes that call for a large quantity of eggs, like quiche. To substitute for one egg, whip ¼ cup of silken tofu and blend it into your recipe.[40,41]

Bananas can be a substitute for one egg. Mash a medium-sized banana before combining it with the other ingredients. Bananas have great moisture content and nutrient value. The more ripe the banana, the sweeter the taste will be. This will in turn affect the sweetness of your recipe.

Pureed Fruit or Vegetables make fantastic low-fat egg replacements, but you'll have to leave this one up to trial and error if you're replacing more than two eggs. I once tried to use applesauce and bananas in a recipe instead of 4 eggs and it was a disaster. Use 3 tablespoons of vegetable or fruit puree per egg.

Fruits and Veggies Pulling Double Duty

Veggies are generally thought of as a traditional side dish and fruit as a stand-alone dessert. But there are so many versatile ways to eat these wonderful rainbow-colored nutrient-rich foods if just you take the time to think outside the box. Here are a few suggestions:

Cauliflower is a fantastic substitute for mashed potatoes, rice, beans for chili or stews, pizza crust, dinner biscuits or gravy. (See Grain-Free Veggie Pizza with Pesto Sauce & Cauliflower Crust, p. 42 and Cauliflower Rice, p. 65). My veggie-packed gluten-free pizza crust includes just a few simple ingredients: cauliflower, flax meal, egg, spices and oil. The biscuits that I like to make have similar ingredients to the pizza crust, but they are baked in muffin tins. Gravy is made by boiling cauliflower in chicken or vegetable stock along with seasonings and onion, then processing the vegetables in a blender while adding some of the stock until the desired consistency is reached.

Zucchini can be used to replace lasagna noodles and other types of pasta, pizza crusts and wraps. Noodles can be made with a vegetable spiralizer, or just a regular vegetable peeler. (See Zucchini Ribbon Salad, p. 63). Wraps are made by blending raw, chopped zucchini in a blender with flax meal and spices, then drying in a food dehydrator. Making a pizza crust entails shredding the zucchini and mixing it with flax meal or gluten-free flour, egg and spices. Zucchini has a high water content. For many recipes it is important to let the zucchini drain or the final product will turn out soggy. I found this out the hard way. After cutting or shredding, set the zucchini aside for 10-15 minutes, then place it in a piece of cheesecloth or a clean dishtowel before squeezing out the excess water.

Sweet Potatoes are no longer just for the holidays. I used to hate sweet potatoes because the only time they were served in my house growing up was on Thanksgiving, with melted marshmallows and brown sugar on top. I could feel a cavity coming on just looking at them. The first time I ate a baked sweet potato as an adult, I fell in love with them. Now I like to serve them mashed, oven roasted, cut into french fries or added to soups. I even mix them with regular mashed potatoes for an extra treat. (See Dairy-Free Mashed Sweet Potatoes, p. 60 and Oven-Roasted Sweet Potatoes, p. 62). Sweet potatoes are packed full of nutritional benefits. They are a good source of vitamins A and C, along with a host of other vitamins. They even have antioxidant properties.[42]

Spaghetti Squash served in place of pasta pairs well with tomato, alfredo or pesto sauce. Add a few other vegetables and meatballs to the sauce for a satisfying meal.

Bananas are such a versatile fruit! They can be used to make a frozen non-dairy dessert similar to frozen yogurt, flourless pancakes, breads and cookies, and to add sweetness and texture to other dishes. (See Flourless Pancakes, p. 71 and Frosty Banana Pudding, p. 90).

Pumpkin Puree can be used to flavor pancakes, cookies, breads and pastries, chili, protein shakes and more. (See Punkin' Chunkin' Cookie Bars, p. 82 and Coconut Pumpkin/Apple Spice Waffles, p. 72).

Applesauce holds its own as a side dish, but it can also be used in pancakes, breads, cookies and pastries to add moisture when replacing eggs or oil, and for taste as well. (See Coconut Pumpkin/Apple Spice Waffles, p. 72).

Plantains, a member of the banana family, are a fruit that looks like oversized bananas. Until they turn yellow, they are more starchy than sweet. Unlike regular bananas, they're not very palatable when eaten raw. Brown plantains are overripe and soft, perfect for use in sweet dishes. Yellow plantains are semi-firm and can be used in recipes like my SB&J Plantain Roll-Ups, (p. 85) by tossing in a blender or food processor with a few other ingredients. Green plantains are used more for drying and grinding into flour for crepes, crackers, or other recipe favorites in place of flour.

To make plantain flour, slice green plantains into approximately ¼-inch chips and bake in a 200°F oven for approximately two hours. Cool, then grind to a powder in a food processor. Two plantains make approximately one cup of flour. You can also purchase this type of flour at some health food stores and online.

Finding plantains in regular grocery stores can sometimes be a challenge. I have found them in a few health food stores but they are most readily available in Latin American markets, as they are traditionally used in this type of cuisine. Prices can vary drastically, depending on the market. I have read blog posts by people who have paid as little as fifteen cents, ranging all the way up to seventy-nine cents per plantain.[43]

Alternatives to Grain Buns, Wraps & Crackers

As a society, our eating habits are so traditional that we almost have to use bread as the foundation for our sandwiches, burgers, wraps, or even the cracker base of our appetizers. With a little creativity, many healthy substitutions are available right in our own kitchens. This works especially well during the summer when it is grilling and burger time for many people. With the farmers' markets in full swing during the summer months, there are so many vegetables to choose from.

A few bun[44] and cracker replacements are as follows:

- Cut whole tomatoes in half and use the top and bottom for buns. If they are too thick, cut an additional slice away from each cut section, leaving the top and bottom ends intact to hold onto. It is best to use room temperature tomatoes since these are a little easier to eat. If tomatoes are large, cut in half for ease of handling after loading with that burger and toppings.

- Cucumbers and zucchini cut lengthwise work well as a substitute for buns or sandwich bread, and they are so delicious! These can also be used as the cracker base for an appetizer by slicing thin with a veggie peeler or slicer and using the thin sheets to wrap around other veggies or even meats like bacon, meatballs or mini sausages.
- Cherry tomatoes or medium-sized tomatoes and cremini mushroom tops can all be used as an appetizer base.
- Portobello mushrooms make great hamburger bun substitutes. Just wash, pat dry and brush both sides with olive oil. Just before the burgers are ready, lightly grill the mushrooms.
- Celery boats can hold ham, chicken, tuna or egg salad. They are also great vehicles for nut and seed butters, making for a delicious high-protein snack.
- Gluten-free wraps have recently gained popularity. Lettuce, the old standby for sandwiches and burgers, can actually be used in place of bread and buns. I buy large-leaf lettuce so there is plenty of room for whatever goodies I want to pack inside. Many people like to use the large leaves of mustard greens. I find these are a bit tough when raw, so I like to sauté them first.
- Flour-based wraps are another option. If you do not want to make gluten-free flour wraps from scratch, there are a few brands available in health food stores. I have used rice wraps and coconut wraps made by Udi's, Rudi's and Gluten Freeda. Store bought wraps can be full of preservatives. The only wraps I have made are the ones found in my SB&J Plantain Roll-Ups (p. 85). These are made with the still wildly underutilized fruit known as plantains (the oversized-looking bananas). I have yet to make wraps with plantain flour or other gluten-free flours.
- Crackers can be substituted with gluten-free options as well, commonly found in health food stores and made by various vendors. Just be sure to read the ingredient labels to assure nothing has been added that will cause you an allergic reaction. Again, watch out for the preservatives and additives often found in store bought goods...just sayin'. Though I have not baked my own gluten-free crackers, there are many fantastic recipes out there.[45]
- For those of you who feel you simply must have some type of bread, but grain is restricted from your diet, Coconut Flour Biscuits (p. 78) can be a good substitute. Based on another recipe that I originally found online[46], I have made them and liked them so

much that I had to include my recipe in the book. Actually, I am eating one as I type this, topped with homemade blueberry jam, and it is delicious! The batter for these biscuits can be made into a loaf of bread as well. This bread does taste like coconut so it might not be the best flavor buddy for the typical savory foods you might eat with biscuits or bread, but it gets my vote.

- Grain-Free Sweet Potato Biscuits (p. 80) are also a favorite of mine. They don't taste like sweet potatoes, and pair well with a dinner, served for breakfast, or just on their own for a snack.

So be bold, live it up and try some new, out-of-the-box ideas for substituting your sandwich bread in a much healthier way. The possibilities are endless and it just takes a little creativity. If you make them yourself, you will know they are not full of preservatives or artificial additives.

5) CONVENIENT KITCHEN TIPS & TOOLS

Until a few years ago, I was never very excited about cooking. Part of this may have been due to the fact that my pantry was never very organized, I didn't know many shortcuts, and I didn't have many tools and gadgets to make life easier. I know most of you don't have time to spend long hours in the kitchen cooking, or agonizing over what to make for meals with all of the food restrictions you or a family member may have encountered. Over the years, I have found tips and tools that have actually made cooking easier as well as enjoyable, and I'm excited to share them with you.

TIPS

- **Keep a variety of fresh fruits and veggies on hand.** Vegetables are helpful for throwing together omelets, casseroles, stir-fry, or a quick meal on the fly. Fruits are nice to have ready for a snack when your sweet tooth comes calling. Frozen fruits and veggies work well too, but you are more apt to grab a quick nutritious snack if it is fresh and cut up instead of frozen.
- **Keep a well-stocked pantry**. It has taken me awhile, but I try to keep my cabinets stocked with ingredients I use often so that if I decide to make something on a whim, I already have the ingredients on hand. I use lots of gluten-free flours, herbs, eggs and coconut aminos, just to name a few.
- **Shop online**. Many hard-to-find items such as coconut aminos, pure vanilla powder,[47] organic gelatin, psyllium husk powder and arrowroot powder are not always available in my nearest health

food store. It can be cheaper for me to purchase a few items online than the cost of gas would be to make a trip to the big health food store a couple hours away.

- Some regular grocery stores sell specialty ingredients such as gluten-free flours and organic items. **Watch for sales!** If you live near discount stores like Big Lots or Marc's, they will sometimes carry gluten-free flours and some organic items a few bucks cheaper than health food or regular grocery stores.

- **Strain the vegetables first** when using cauliflower or zucchini in casseroles, or to replace noodles in a dish that will be baked. Place cut or shredded vegetables in a strainer, sprinkle with salt, and let them sit for at least 10 minutes. These particular veggies naturally contain a significant amount of water that will make your baked dishes soupy if you do not do this step first. Press the veggies in the strainer to remove some of the water, then wrap them in a dishtowel and squeeze out the remaining excess water.

- **Parchment paper is a must have!** I line baking sheets, baking dishes, muffin tins or anywhere that I don't want to have a big mess to clean up.

- **Don't throw away your gluten-free bread ends** if no one likes to use them for toast. Keep in the freezer until you have enough to make breadcrumbs. Place in a blender or food processor to chop up, then throw in a skillet or low-temperature oven to brown. Add your favorite herbs and spices.

- Have you ever made a homemade loaf of bread that just didn't turn out the way you wanted it to? You can **recycle your flopped bread** by crumbling and placing in the freezer to use later in meatloaf or meatballs, or to make breadcrumbs as described above.

- To **remove any lingering garlic odor from your hands**, simply rub them on stainless steel (like your kitchen faucet) and the smell will be eliminated.

- **Cook in batches to save time!** Planning ahead is essential for people with busy lifestyles who want to make nutritious meals for themselves and their families at home, whether you are working with an allergy-driven diet full of ingredient substitutions or not. When it comes to planning meals, I like to think ahead and do "batch cooking." For example, I like to cook extra chicken, cauliflower, rice, quinoa or potatoes so I will have enough leftovers or prepared raw ingredients to make several recipes for later in the week. Also, if I am going to need extra veggies chopped for other recipes during the week, I will clean and prep them ahead of time and keep them in containers in the fridge for when I need them.

This is great for days when you are short on time. I like to do my batch cooking every Sunday, making up meals that freeze well and popping them in the slow cooker before heading out for the day or right before entering dreamland at night.

Common Kitchen Measurement Conversions[48]

1 tablespoon (tbsp.) =	3 teaspoons (tsp.)
1/16 cup =	1 tablespoon
1/8 cup =	2 tablespoons
1/6 cup =	2 tablespoons + 2 teaspoons
1/4 cup =	4 tablespoons
1/3 cup =	5 tablespoons + 1 teaspoon
3/8 cup =	6 tablespoons
1/2 cup =	8 tablespoons
2/3 cup =	10 tablespoons + 2 teaspoons
3/4 cup =	12 tablespoons
1 cup =	48 teaspoons or 16 tablespoons
1 fluid ounce =	2 tablespoons
8 fluid ounces =	1 cup
1 pint (pt.) =	2 cups
1 quart (qt.) =	2 pints
4 cups =	1 quart
1 gallon (gal.) =	4 quarts
16 ounces (oz.) =	1 pound (lb.)

TRICKS

- An ice cube tray works well for freezing unused portions of many things. I like to freeze leftover fresh herbs by washing and chopping them, dividing them among the sections of an ice cube tray, then filling the rest of the way with water and freezing. Other leftovers that freeze well are chicken or beef broth, pumpkin puree, tomato sauce and tomato paste. Once frozen, I pop the cubes into a freezer bag and label it. This makes it more convenient for future uses and cuts down on food waste.

- If your blender is easy to clean, use it to mix up batters instead of stirring by hand.

- If a recipe calls for room temperature eggs but you just don't have the time to wait, cold eggs can be brought to room temperature by placing in a bowl of warm water for 5-10 minutes.

- Need oat flour but don't have any? Save an unwanted trip to the store by placing uncooked old fashioned oats in the blender and processing until it reaches the consistency of flour.

- Peel bananas upside-down to eliminate the strings.

- If you are making waffles, pancakes, or french toast for a crowd, keep them warm without getting soggy on the bottom by placing a wire cooling rack on top of a baking sheet. Put the waffles or pancakes on the cooling rack and keep them warm in a 200°F oven for up to 25 minutes (any longer and they tend to dry out). Any type of wire or ovenproof rack will work.

- A zipper-topped plastic bag with one of the corners cut off can be used to drizzle icing over rolls, or you can make the hole bigger for filling deviled eggs if you don't have a pastry bag handy.

TOOLS

- **Blender-** Ninja or any easy-to-clean blender. I have a Ninja that is almost worn out because I use it so much. The blades pull right out and come apart for easy cleaning. I use it to make sauces, stews and soups, and for

- mixing most batters, including pancake and waffle batter. I even use it to mash potatoes. It is such a time saver!

- **Apple Slicer-** We eat a lot of apples at my house and I also make Nut-Free Baked Apples (p. 91) and Cinnamon Stovetop Apples (p. 92) quite often. What a time saver this less than $5 device is!

- **Glass Measuring Bowls** of various sizes- I am all about glass when it comes to mixing and storing foods. I love the ease of cleanup, plus not having to worry about chemicals leaching out into the food as can happen with plastic.

- **Silicon Spatulas** are very flexible and will conform to the container you are trying to clean out. I have various sizes from small to large.

- **Nu-Wave Oven-** I cook sooo many things in this countertop infrared gadget. I love being able to take chicken or fish directly from the freezer to the oven and not having to wait for it to thaw. It's also great for cooking hamburgers and roasted veggies, drying herbs, and even making desserts. I have made cakes, cookies and quick breads using this device. Even my Pork-N-Broccoli Tater Skins (p. 53) are great in the Nu-Wave Oven.
- **Knives-** Sharp knives in various sizes are a must in the kitchen! I have my favorite large stainless steel chef's knife, plus several ceramic knives in different sizes.
- **Pots & Pans-** Stainless steel is a must in my kitchen for cookware. I have eliminated aluminum cookware as much as possible, due to the potential harmful effects aluminum can have on the body. My two favorite go-to pot sizes are the 2-quart and 3-quart with glass lids. I also have a large stockpot for stews and bigger items.
- **Cast Iron-** I have three different sizes of cast iron skillets, plus a cast iron griddle. Mine are the old style without the ceramic coating. Although I am not a big fan of the cleanup required after use, I do like the even heating that they offer, plus the ability to use them in the oven for making roasted veggies. Cast iron can also bake up a mean batch of cornbread if you are a die-hard cornbread fan.
- **Baking Dishes-** I try to use glass or ceramic whenever possible. If I am forced to use aluminum pans, I always line them with parchment paper.
- **Cooling racks** are handy items for cooling cookies and baked goods. I even like to sit hot pans on them. I have a small square and a larger rectangular size that's big enough to hold a 13x9" pan. It is also good size for cooling when making several batches of cookies.
- **Spiral Veggie Slicer-** A non-electric gadget that's handy for cutting veggies into spirals, for grating, and to make long, thin noodles from zucchini and other vegetables. Also known as a spiralizer.
- **Slow Cookers** in various sizes can be useful, depending on the type of dishes you are preparing or the size of your family. I have three sizes that I call the daddy, momma, and baby size. I do a lot of overnight cooking of meats, stews and soups in these.
- **Cutting Boards** in various sizes are useful for everything from peeling and slicing small items to larger jobs, like when I am cutting many veggies for stir-fry. I only use wood cutting boards and I

have three sizes, but others prefer plastic or glass. My mom has a plastic cutting board that has been used so much the plastic flakes off, but she doesn't like wood. There is much debate over which type of cutting board holds less bacteria. I have looked at several sources and it's not surprising that the opinions differ.[49]

6) MAIN DISHES

Grain-Free Veggie Pizza with Pesto Sauce & Cauliflower Crust

I absolutely love pizza, but with my dietary restrictions I haven't had a regular pizza in years. It's nice to be able to come up with substitutions that meet that need. I have experimented with various vegetables as a crust and so far this has worked the best for me. This pizza crust could even stand up to a regular pizza sauce in moderation, as long as the crust was baked to a deep golden brown. Just like regular pizza, the topping choices are endless. Don't be afraid to be creative!

This recipe was adapted from and inspired by Lauren Goslin, Oatmealwithafork.com.

Serves 1-2

PESTO
- 1 cup fresh basil, stems removed
- 1 cup fresh oregano, stems removed
- ¼ cup raw unsalted pumpkin seeds
- ¼ cup raw unsalted sunflower seeds
- 3 cloves garlic
- ½ cup olive oil
- 2 tablespoons nutritional yeast
- Salt and pepper to taste

Combine all of the ingredients in a blender until well blended, scraping the sides a couple of times as you go. This makes a larger batch than you will need for a single pizza, but leftover pesto can be frozen in ice cube trays for use in later recipes.

PIZZA CRUST
- 2 cups cauliflower
- 2 large eggs
- 2 teaspoons olive oil
- 2 tablespoons water
- 2 teaspoon nutritional yeast
- ¼ teaspoon dried oregano

- ¼ teaspoon dried basil
- ¼ teaspoon garlic powder
- ¼ teaspoon sea salt
- ½ cup flax meal, divided

TOPPINGS
- 2-3 tablespoons pesto
- Your favorite veggies, sliced

1) Place cauliflower in a blender or food processor in small batches, pulsing until it reaches a rice-like consistency. Be careful not to over process.

2) In a small saucepan, bring water to a boil. Turn off the heat and add the cauliflower to the pan. Cover and let stand for approximately 10 minutes.

3) Transfer cauliflower to a mesh strainer set over the sink or a bowl to cool, then press to remove excess moisture.

4) While the cauliflower continues to drain, preheat oven to 400°F. In a bowl, combine all of the remaining ingredients except ¼ cup of the flax meal. Set aside.

5) Remove cauliflower from strainer and place on a clean dishtowel. Wrap a clean dishtowel around the cauliflower and squeeze out any excess moisture that remains.

6) Add cauliflower to the mixture that you set aside, stirring to blend well. Slowly add the remaining ¼ cup of flax meal. Dough should be sticky, not runny. To thicken, add more flax meal 1 tablespoon at a time.

7) Line a round 12" or larger pizza pan or stone with parchment paper coated with olive or coconut oil.

8) With well-oiled hands or wearing food grade gloves, spread dough out onto the parchment paper to about cracker thickness. Dough that is spread out too thickly will result in a pizza that is soggy in the middle.

9) Bake for approximately 35 minutes or until top starts to brown. At this point, carefully turn dough over by placing parchment paper on top to flip. Return to the oven and continue to bake until the dough starts to brown, about 10 minutes.

10) Remove pizza from the oven and increase oven temperature to 450°F.

11) Cover pizza with a thin layer of pesto

12) Add your favorite veggie toppings. I like to use sliced cherry tomatoes, mushrooms, green and red bell peppers, artichoke hearts (drained), black olives, fresh basil and spinach topped with Daiya dairy-free mozzarella cheese. Keep moist toppings like tomatoes and artichokes to a minimum so the pizza does not become soggy.

13) Place pizza back in the oven until the cheese starts to melt. If you are not using cheese, bake until toppings are warmed through.

14) Cut and serve immediately.

No-Bean Chili (a.k.a. Paleo Chili)

Cauliflower is used to replace the beans in this chili, but almost any vegetable that doesn't turn mushy can be used. It's not that I have anything against beans, but dietary restrictions sometimes call for a creative substitution and cauliflower holds up well. Chili always tastes best to me on cold, rainy days, especially if it was made the day before, as the flavor is better the second day.

Yield: 4-6 bowls

- 1-2 cups chopped cauliflower
- 2 tablespoons ghee, butter or coconut oil
- 2 lbs. grass-fed ground beef
- 1 medium onion, diced
- 3-4 cloves garlic, minced
- ½ cup carrots, cut into matchsticks
- 2 stalks celery, diced
- ½ red bell pepper, diced
- ½ green bell pepper, diced
- 2 15-ounce cans diced tomatoes
- 1 6-ounce can tomato paste
- 1 tablespoon raw honey
- 1-2 teaspoons chili powder, or more to taste

1) Rinse cauliflower and place a few pieces at a time in the blender or food processor until chopped into small pieces, a little bigger than rice but not so small that they turn into crumbs. Set aside.

2) Heat the ghee, butter or coconut oil in a skillet and add the cauliflower.

3) Sautee approximately 5 minutes, then set aside

4) Brown ground beef in the same skillet.

5) Once most of the beef has cooked, add onions and garlic. Continue cooking until rest of meat has browned.

6) Add carrots, celery and peppers. Mix well.

7) Add the tomatoes and tomato paste and continue cooking on medium heat.

8) Add honey and mix well.

9) Add chili powder and continue to simmer for 5-10 minutes for the powder to become distributed and the flavor to blend in.

10) Add the cauliflower and continue cooking for 10 more minutes or until cauliflower softens but not so long that it becomes mushy.

Chicken Chili

Some people refer to chili without tomato sauce as white chili. Since mine contains chicken, I call it as chicken chili. This is another warming dish that's perfect to serve on a cold or rainy day. Celery and carrots are added as flavor, color and nutrition enhancers.

Yield: 4-6 bowls

- 1 lb. dried great northern beans
- 3 cups chicken broth
- 2 cups water
- 1 medium onion
- 2 stalks celery
- 1 large carrot
- 2 tablespoons olive oil
- 2 boneless skinless chicken breasts
- 1 teaspoon garlic powder
- 1 teaspoon sea salt
- 1 teaspoon black pepper
- 1 tablespoon fresh basil, chopped
- 1 tablespoon fresh oregano, stems removed
- 1 large leaf fresh kale, stem removed

1) The day before you're planning to serve this chili, sort through the dried beans, picking out any dark or discolored beans along with any small rocks.

2) Rinse beans thoroughly and then cover with fresh water. Cover with plastic wrap or a lid and soak at least over night. The beans will expand, so make sure they are covered with plenty of water.

3) The next day, drain the beans, rinse, and place in a large slow cooker. Cover with the chicken broth, making sure the beans are fully covered. If not, add some of the water.

4) Chop onion and add to the beans. If you're going to be at home, turn slow cooker on high for approximately 4 hours and cook until beans are semi-soft. If not, cook on low approximately 6 hours.

5) Chop celery and carrot into bite-sized pieces and add to the slow cooker.

6) If chicken is thick, use a meat mallet on more dense areas to help shorten cooking time.

7) Cut chicken into bite-sized pieces. In a large skillet, heat olive oil on medium high. Once oil is hot but before it begins smoking, add chicken and brown.

8) Transfer chicken to the slow cooker.

9) Add garlic powder, salt, pepper, chopped basil and oregano, and finish cooking for approximately 1 hour or until beans are soft. Tear kale into bite-sized pieces and add to the chili just before serving.

Crowd-Pleasing Grain-Free Slow Cooker Meatballs

This recipe is great for a potluck dinner, tailgating party, meatball sub night or spaghetti night. I have made these meatballs in the slow cooker without browning first, but they just taste better when they're browned in a skillet with a little oil first. If I have any leftover pepper bacon grease to brown them in, the flavor is really enhanced. I think these taste better the second day, as most tomato-based dishes do, but in my house, it is difficult to find any uneaten meatballs that made it to the second day.

Yield: 20-25 meatballs

- 2 cloves garlic
- 1 large stalk celery
- 1 large carrot (or pulp saved from juicing)
- 1 small onion
- ¼ green or red bell pepper (optional)
- 1lb. grass-fed ground beef
- 1 lb. ground sausage (I prefer mild, but spicy works too)
- 1 egg
- 1 tablespoon flax meal, more as needed
- 1 tablespoon fresh basil (or 1 teaspoon dried)
- 1 tablespoon fresh oregano (or 1 teaspoon dried)
- ½ teaspoon sea salt
- ½ teaspoon pepper
- 2-4 tablespoons coconut or olive oil
- About 24 oz. of your favorite tomato sauce

1) In a food processor or blender/chopper, mince garlic, celery, carrot, onion and peppers. Set aside.

2) In large bowl, combine the beef and sausage with your hands until well mixed.

3) Combine meat mixture with the minced vegetables and all of the remaining ingredients except the oil and tomato sauce. If mixture is too wet, add enough additional flax meal for the meatballs to hold together.

4) Portion meat mixture with a small ice cream scoop and roll into balls. Refrigerate for a few hours.

5) Remove from fridge and preheat oil in a large skillet. Brown meatballs, pushing them around the skillet for even browning.

6) Coat the bottom of the slow cooker with a small amount of sauce. Add a layer of meatballs and cover with more sauce, continuing to add meatballs and sauce in alternating layers until you've added all the meatballs. Finish with a final covering of sauce. Cook on low for approximately 4-6 hours, or until the meatballs are cooked through.

Soy-Free Chicken & Veggie Stir-Fry

I didn't prepare stir-fry at home for a long time since I am allergic to soy and couldn't find a suitable replacement for soy sauce... and then I discovered coconut aminos. This product, made from organic coconut sap and sea salt, is a great alternative to soy sauce.

Although I include specific veggies in this recipe, it's just as easy to use whatever your favorite combination might be. Serve alone or on top of rice, pasta or veggie pasta.

Serves 2-3

- 2 heads broccoli
- ½ head cauliflower
- 2-3 cloves garlic
- 2 leftover grilled or sautéed chicken breasts, or 2 boneless skinless chicken breasts
- 1-2 tablespoons coconut oil
- ½ cup chicken broth
- ¼ cup coconut aminos
- 1 small onion, chopped
- 2 carrots, cut into matchsticks
- 2 stalks celery, sliced thin
- 1 tablespoon cornstarch or arrowroot powder

1) Chop broccoli and cauliflower into bite-sized pieces and mince the garlic. Cut chicken into thin strips. If you're using raw chicken, heat the coconut oil in a skillet. Cook approximately 5-6 minutes or until juices run clear, then set aside.

2) Place chicken broth and coconut aminos in skillet over medium heat.

3) Add all veggies and cover, continuing to cook for approximately 8-10 minutes or until crispy tender. Remove from skillet using a slotted spoon so most of the cooking liquid remains in the pan.

4) Add cornstarch or arrowroot powder to 2 tablespoons of cold water and stir until completely dissolved. Add to the skillet, stirring until thickened. If the sauce gets too thick, add more coconut aminos to thin it out and add flavor.

5) Add veggies and chicken back to the pan and stir until coated with the sauce.

Pork-N-Broccoli Tater Skins

Potato skins are a popular appetizer on many restaurant menus. The problem for me is that they always contain real cheese. This recipe is fun to make if you're looking for a dairy-free dish that's different. This recipe incorporates meat and veggies and could even be served as a meal instead of an appetizer. If broccoli is not your thing, it may be substituted with another veggie such as green beans or even steamed cauliflower.

Yield: 12 potato skins

- 2-3 lb. pork roast[50]
- Olive oil or coconut oil
- 3-4 ounces of your favorite BBQ sauce (optional)
- 3 large baking potatoes
- 3 medium sweet potatoes
- Coarse sea salt
- 1 large head broccoli
- 1 cup shredded cheddar Daiya or other cheese substitute

1) Brown pork roast on all sides in a skillet coated with oil or on the grill. Place in a slow cooker with 1 cup of water. Cook on low for 6-8 hours.

2) Once pork is cooked, shred and add your favorite BBQ sauce if desired.

3) Preheat oven to 450°F. Scrub the potatoes well and cut off any bad spots. Dry with a paper towel.

4) Coat potato skins with olive oil or coconut oil, then sprinkle with coarse sea salt.

5) Place potatoes on a wire rack and bake 45-60 minutes. The sweet potatoes will cook a little faster than the white potatoes. Cooking times will vary depending on the size of potatoes as well, so prick potatoes with a fork to test for doneness. Potatoes can also be baked in the Nu-Wave Oven on full power for approximately 45 minutes.

6) After removing potatoes from the oven, preheat the broiler. Cut potatoes lengthwise and carefully scoop out the centers, leaving a small amount of potato around the sides and bottoms. (You can use the leftover potato to make Dairy-Free Mashed Potatoes (p. 60) to go with the leftover pork for the next night's meal).

7) Rub inside of potato skins with a little olive or coconut oil and recoat the outside if needed. Place under the broiler on a wire rack or in your Nu-Wave Oven for approximately 5-10 minutes, just long enough to make them a little crispy.

8) While potatoes are crisping, boil a small amount of water in a pot fitted with a vegetable steamer and tight-fitting lid. Chop broccoli into small pieces and steam for 5 minutes, then drain.

9) Sprinkle half the cheese substitute equally among the potato skins, then top with the desired amount of pork and broccoli. Sprinkle the top of each potato with the remaining cheese.

10) Place back under the broiler (or in Nu-Wave Oven) long enough to melt the cheese.

Grain-Free Marzetti

One thing that I miss from my grade school days is the marzetti casserole that we used to get for lunch in the cafeteria. For anyone on a grain-free diet, veggies can become your pasta noodles. This recipe can also be made with cooked gluten-free noodles instead, by omitting the cauliflower and zucchini.

Serves 2-3

- 1 cup grated cauliflower and/or zucchini
- ½ teaspoon salt
- 1 lb. ground beef or ground turkey
- ½ onion, chopped
- 2 cloves garlic, chopped (or 1 teaspoon garlic powder)
- 2 stalks celery, chopped
- 1 15-oz. can diced tomatoes
- 4 ounces (approximately ½ small can) tomato sauce
- 1 6-ounce can tomato paste
- ½ green bell pepper, diced
- 1 teaspoon dried basil
- 1 teaspoon dried oregano
- 1 cup shredded cheddar Daiya or other cheese substitute
- Salt and pepper to taste

1) Preheat oven to 350°F.

2) Place the cauliflower and/or zucchini in a strainer placed over the sink or a dish. Sprinkle with salt. Let sit approximately 10-15 minutes. The salt will help bring the moisture out of the cauliflower and zucchini quickly.

3) While it's still in the strainer, push the cauliflower and/or zucchini with your hands a few times to squeeze out any excess water.

4) Brown the ground beef or turkey in a skillet. Just before it is totally browned, add the onion, garlic, and celery.

5) Add the diced tomatoes, tomato sauce, tomato paste, green pepper, basil and oregano. Let simmer for a few minutes.

6) Place cauliflower and/or zucchini in a clean dishtowel, squeezing over the sink to get out the remaining water.

7) Add zucchini and/or or cauliflower to the skillet and stir to combine. Mixture should be thick.

8) Spoon half of the mixture into a 2-quart casserole dish. Top with half of the cheese.

9) Spoon the remaining mixture on top and finish with the remaining cheese. (If you are a big cheese fan then by all means, load up with more!).

10) Bake uncovered for approximately 30-40 minutes, checking after 15-20 minutes to see if the mixture has become soupy. If it has, use a large spoon or ladle to dip out some of the excess liquid. Continue cooking until the cheese on top is nice and bubbly.

11) Cool for a few minutes and add salt and pepper to taste before serving.

Easy-Peasy Roast Dinner with Flavor Poppin' Mashed Potatoes

A hearty roast dinner takes me back to when I was growing up, when the roast would be baking in mom's oven on Sunday morning for several hours. Since then, the slow cooker has become a big part of my kitchen, especially when it comes to cooking roasts. The tender perfection of the meat and the savory flavor of the cooked vegetables and mashed potatoes are so amazing, and I love knowing that dinner is cooking while I sleep. Home cooking doesn't get much easier than this.

Serves 4-6

- 1-2 tablespoons coconut oil
- 1 4-6 lb. beef roast
- Salt and pepper to taste
- 5-6 medium potatoes
- Small onion
- 1 lb. baby carrots
- 1-2 cups water

1) In large skillet heat the oil. While the skillet is heating, rub the roast all over with salt and pepper, then brown the roast on all sides. I sometimes brown the roast on the grill for less mess, especially when I take it directly from the freezer without waiting for it to thaw first.

2) While the meat is browning, scrub the potatoes and cut out any bad spots or eyes.

3) Chop the onion and place it along with the carrots and potatoes in a large slow cooker.

4) Add water to cover. This will help to keep the vegetables from turning dark. Place the roast on top of the veggies and cook on low for 6-8 hours or overnight. Roast should fall apart easily.

5) Transfer roast to a platter for serving. Serve the carrots directly from the slow cooker or place in another serving dish.

6) Place potatoes in a large mixing bowl. Mash potatoes with mixer on low until blended into smaller chunks, then beat in broth from the roast ½ cup at a time on high, being careful not to add too much. You still want the potatoes to have a thick consistency, so avoid making them too runny. Like the Fonz said on *Happy Days*, "Oh, hey, these are great mashed potatoes, Mrs. Cunningham... Yeah, I mean good and stiff, just like they make at the diner."[51] (Okay, I am showing my age here).

7) Add salt and pepper to taste.

7) SIDE DISHES

Dairy-Free Mashed Sweet Potatoes

Move over white potatoes, there's a more colorful side dish taking over! Sweet potatoes are not just for the holidays anymore. I actually like to blend these with regular mashed potatoes for a unique taste that combines the best of both worlds, served with buttery-flavored ghee or coconut butter.

Serves 4-6

- 5-6 medium sweet potatoes
- 4-½ cups chicken broth, divided
- Salt and pepper to taste
- Ghee or coconut butter to taste (optional)
- Raw honey to taste (optional)

1) Wash the potatoes thoroughly and cut out any bad spots, then cut into chunks. Peels can be removed, if you prefer, but they add a significant vitamin boost!

2) Add potatoes to a pot along with 4 cups of chicken broth. Add enough water to cover the potatoes if needed.

3) Boil potatoes until tender, approximately 20-25 minutes.

4) Once potatoes are tender, drain and transfer to a blender or large bowl. Whip in small batches or beat with an electric mixer, adding the reserved ½ cup of chicken broth a little at a time to reach the desired consistency. Sweet potatoes mash to a thinner consistency than white potatoes, so be careful not to add too much liquid.

5) Season to taste with salt and pepper. You can also add ghee, coconut butter or honey to taste, or any other seasonings and condiments that you like with your sweet potatoes.

Pepper Bacon Mashed Tater Cakes

Leftover mashed potatoes can sometimes be a little boring reheated on their own. This recipe, made with pepper bacon, puts these leftovers in a class of their own. These cakes can be served as a sidekick at breakfast or for dinner. Be creative by adding any of your favorite ingredients, like chopped asparagus, spinach, non-dairy cheese or mushrooms. The possibilities are endless.

Serves 4-6

- 2 cups mashed potatoes (perhaps leftover from Easy-Peasy Roast Dinner with Flavor Poppin' Mashed Potatoes, p. 57)
- 1 egg
- 6-8 pieces pepper bacon, cooked and crumbled, drippings reserved
- 2 tablespoons gluten-free flour
- 1 teaspoon dehydrated onion flakes
- 1 teaspoon garlic powder

1) Combine potatoes with the egg and mix well.

2) Add all remaining ingredients except the bacon drippings and stir. Mixture should be thick enough to form into balls just a little smaller than baseball size, using a heaping ¼ cup of the mixture per ball. If mixture is too thin, add extra flour 1 tablespoon at a time.

3) Heat the leftover bacon drippings or your favorite oil in a large skillet on medium-high heat. To make sure the oil is hot enough, drop a small amount of potato in the skillet to make sure it sizzles. The cakes will absorb the oil, creating wonderful flavor! Form mixture into balls and place as many in the hot skillet as will fit, leaving room to flatten each into a patty. You may need to oil your spatula before pressing down as these will stick.

4) Brown 3-5 minutes per side, flipping only once.

Oven-Roasted Sweet Potatoes

These potatoes are always a hit in my household. Since these potatoes tend to shrink up during the cooking process, I always make more than I think I'll need. They taste just as good as leftovers. Sweet potatoes are powerhouses of vitamins and nutrients and serve as a great inflammation fighter in our intestinal tract.

Rather than roasting these potatoes on a baking sheet, I sometimes like to bake them in a preheated cast iron skillet that gets them nice and brown. I also occasionally bake these in my Nu-Wave Oven, which only takes 20-25 minutes. This recipe can also be used for baking new potatoes or white potatoes.

- 1 large or 2 small sweet potatoes per person
- 2 tablespoons olive oil
- Seasonings, according to taste (optional)

1) Preheat oven to 400°F.

2) Cut potatoes into small wedges.

3) Place potatoes in a plastic bag and add the olive oil. Shake bag to coat the potatoes well.

4) Spread potatoes out in a single layer on a baking sheet.

5) Sprinkle with your favorite seasonings (sea salt, seasoned salt, paprika, etc.) and bake for approximately 40-45 minutes, turning over once they start to brown.

Zucchini Ribbon Salad

This makes a great stand-alone salad for lunch or a side dish at dinnertime. Summer is a wonderful time to make this salad, when zucchini, cherry tomatoes, fresh basil and oregano are bountiful.

Serves 4-6

DRESSING

- 1/2 cup extra virgin olive oil
- 2 tablespoons apple cider vinegar (or more to taste)
- ½ teaspoon Dijon mustard (or more to taste)
- 1 tablespoon raw honey
- 1 teaspoon dried oregano
- 1 teaspoon dried basil
- ¼ teaspoon dried thyme
- ¼ teaspoon dried parsley
- 1 teaspoon garlic powder
- 1 teaspoon onion powder
- ½ teaspoon sea salt
- ½ teaspoon ground black pepper

Combine all ingredients in a blender. Add mustard or vinegar according to taste. Set aside.

SALAD MIX

- 3 zucchini
- 1 clove garlic, minced
- ¼ cup chopped fresh basil leaves
- 1 tablespoon nutritional yeast
- ½ cup grape or cherry tomatoes

1) Wash and peel zucchini, leaving some of the peel on to give the ribbons a splash of color.

2) Using a vegetable slicer with a thin blade, make spiral ribbons of zucchini, or use a vegetable peeler to make long ribbon slices the length of the zucchini. Set aside.

3) Wash and halve the tomatoes. Combine with the zucchini ribbons. Add the garlic and basil.

4) Pour enough dressing over the salad mix to coat, being careful not to drench it. Toss to mix.

5) Sprinkle nutritional yeast over the top and place in the fridge for 1-2 hours so the salad can absorb the dressing before serving.

Cauliflower Rice

If you are trying to totally avoid grains, this is a great dish to use for stir-fries, as a side dish, or as a filler in casseroles and chili if you are also trying to cut beans out of your diet. It makes a tasty pizza crust as well.

- 1 head cauliflower
- 4 tablespoons ghee, coconut or olive oil
- Sea salt and pepper

1) Wash cauliflower and drain.

2) Chop cauliflower into pieces that will fit into a food processor or blender. Working in batches, process until cauliflower pieces resemble grains of rice. I like to process the cauliflower in my Ninja blender, but the whole head does not fit. I process in stages, dumping each processed batch into a bowl before adding more so the cauliflower doesn't blend into a fine powder.

3) Once all of the cauliflower has been processed, heat ghee, coconut or olive oil in a large skillet on medium-high heat. Add the cauliflower rice, stirring continuously until it starts to brown, about 5-6 minutes.

4) Remove from skillet and add salt and pepper to taste, tossing to mix well. Serve immediately or add to other dishes.

Savory Mushroom Quinoa

I can't say enough about the many dishes quinoa can be used for. It is a great substitute for rice in Asian cooking or as a side dish. This grain has a very mild, nutty taste on its own, yet it pairs well with just about any ingredients you want to add and it will not overpower the dish. Baby bella mushrooms pair well with quinoa and contain an abundance of nutrient value, including inflammation-fighting properties

Serves 2

- ½ cup quinoa
- 1 cup chicken, beef or veggie broth
- 1-½ cups baby bella (cremini) mushrooms
- 2 cloves garlic, minced
- ¼ cup diced onions
- ¼ cup coconut aminos
- 2 tablespoons ghee, organic butter or coconut oil
- ½ teaspoon sea salt
- ½ teaspoon pepper
- 1 head broccoli (optional)

1) Rinse quinoa well before cooking. Bring broth to a boil.

2) Add quinoa, cover and reduce heat to a simmer for 15-20 minutes or until water is absorbed.

3) While quinoa is cooking, wash and slice mushrooms thin, including the stems. Set aside. Chop broccoli into small florets if you are using it, and set aside in a separate bowl.

4) Melt ghee, butter or coconut oil completely in a large skillet over medium-high heat. Add mushrooms, garlic and onion, stirring occasionally until onions are almost translucent and mushrooms turn a golden brown (5-7 minutes).

5) Add coconut aminos and broccoli and mix well. Simmer approximately five minutes or until liquid has reduced by half and broccoli has warmed through but retains its crunch.

6) Add quinoa to the skillet and stir to coat. Serve immediately.

Oven-Roasted Veggies

There's nothing like adding oven-roasted veggies to a meal during the fall or winter months when it is cold outside, to warm you up inside. These can be eaten as a side dish or as the main dish of a meal. This recipe is so versatile, it can be made using any combination of your favorite root veggies, like parsnips, turnips and beets as well.

Serves 1-2

- 3 tablespoons olive or coconut oil, divided
- 2 large carrots
- 6 large Brussels sprouts
- 1 large sweet potato
- 2 stalks celery
- 1 onion, diced
- 3 cloves garlic, minced
- 1 teaspoon dried rosemary
- 1 teaspoon dried thyme
- 1 teaspoon dried sage
- 1 teaspoon dried oregano
- $\frac{1}{2}$ teaspoon sea salt
- $\frac{1}{2}$ teaspoon pepper

1) Add 1 tablespoon of oil to a large cast iron skillet and place in the oven. Preheat oven to 400°F.

2) Wash and cut veggies into bite-sized pieces and place in a large bowl.

3) Add remaining ingredients to the bowl, stirring well to coat veggies with oil.

4) Pour into the preheated skillet. Return to the oven and cook 35-40 minutes or until veggies begin to caramelize.

8) BREAKFAST DISHES

Breakfast-On-The-Run Oatmeal Bars

With my food restrictions, it's often difficult to find a fiber or protein bar on the market that I can eat. This recipe is a great substitute, without the worry of off-limits ingredients or preservatives I can't even pronounce. Great to grab in the mornings when short on time, or they make a great anytime snack.

Yield: 6-8 bars

- ¼ cup flax meal
- 2 cups gluten-free oats
- 1 teaspoon cinnamon
- ¼ teaspoon nutmeg
- ⅛ teaspoon salt
- 1 room-temperature egg
- ½ cup coconut oil, melted
- ½ cup raw honey
- ½ teaspoon pure vanilla extract
- 1 cup Nut-Free Trail Mix (p. 81) (I like to include ¼ cup dried blueberries in the mix)

1) Preheat oven to 350°F.

2) In a large bowl combine the flax meal, oats, cinnamon, nutmeg and salt. Set aside.

3) In another large bowl, beat egg with electric mixer until frothy. Then mix in the coconut oil, honey and vanilla.

4) Add dry ingredient mixture to the wet ingredients and mix well.

5) Add trail mix and stir to combine. Mixture will be thick.

6) Line an 8x8" glass baking dish with a piece of parchment paper large enough to hang over the sides. Spread mixture evenly in the baking dish.

7) Bake for 30-35 minutes or until golden brown and sides start to pull away from the parchment paper. Cool completely before cutting into squares.

Flourless Pancakes

I have made this recipe many times and I like how quick and easy it is. These pancakes can be eaten plain or served up with your favorite fruit topping or pure maple syrup. For an added dash of flavor, sprinkle a pinch of cinnamon into the mix.

Serves 2

- 2 ripe bananas
- 1 egg
- 2 tablespoons flax meal
- Coconut oil

1) Mix bananas, egg and flax meal in a blender.

2) Coat a large skillet with coconut oil and place over medium-high heat.

3) Place ¼ cup of the mixture in the center of the heated pan. Flip after bubbles form on top of pancake. Continue to cook until cooked through.

Coconut Pumpkin/Apple Spice Waffles

These waffles have become a hit for breakfast around my house. The wonderful smell of cinnamon gets everyone to the table quickly. These taste great topped with fruit, maple syrup or even coconut cream with honey drizzled over the top, but they also taste just as great served plain.

Yield: 8 4x4" waffles

- ½ cup coconut flour
- 1 tablespoon flax meal
- ½ teaspoon baking soda
- 1 tablespoon cinnamon
- ½ teaspoon nutmeg
- ½ teaspoon ground ginger
- ½ cup pumpkin puree or applesauce
- ½ cup coconut milk
- 2 tablespoons coconut oil
- 2 tablespoons raw honey (or more to taste)
- 6 large eggs

1) Combine coconut flour, flax meal, baking soda, cinnamon, nutmeg, and ground ginger in a bowl and set aside.

2) Place pumpkin puree or applesauce, coconut milk, coconut oil, honey and eggs in a blender and blend well.

3) Add dry ingredients to wet and continue blending until well mixed. If batter is too thick, thin down with more coconut milk. I like to make my batter thick as opposed to runny for more dense waffles.

4) Add approximately ¼ cup of batter to each side of a preheated 4x4" waffle iron, evenly distributing the batter. Do not overfill. Cook time on my waffle iron is approximately 3-4 minutes. If you have a larger waffle iron, you will have to increase the amount of batter and possibly the cook time.

Grab-N-Go Egg Bakes

These are great to make in muffin tins since you can tailor each portion to your family's liking. Just remember which ones were made with certain ingredients that a family member might not like!

Yield: 6 muffins

- Bacon, ham or sausage (optional)
- Raw veggies of your choice
- 6 large eggs[52]
- 1 teaspoon garlic powder
- 1 teaspoon onion powder
- ½ teaspoon salt
- ½ teaspoon pepper
- 6 tablespoons shredded cheddar Daiya or other cheese substitute

1) Preheat oven to 350°F.

2) Line a muffin tin with parchment paper or paper muffin liners, or coat well with coconut oil. It wouldn't hurt to also coat the paper liners with oil, as these tend to stick.

3) If using meat as an ingredient, cook first, then shred into pieces.

4) Distribute 1 tablespoon each of meat and vegetables into each section of the muffin tin.

5) Whisk eggs, garlic powder, onion powder, salt and pepper together, then pour over meat and veggies to cover, being careful not to fill above the edge of the liners. Sprinkle with cheese substitute if using.

6) Bake 25-30 minutes or until knife inserted in the center comes out clean.

Quinoa Porridge

There's nothing like a warming bowl of porridge on cool mornings to help warm up the belly. Quinoa is such an easygoing grain that pairs well with just about any ingredients for any type of meal. The cacao powder in this dish is an added treat. This porridge even makes a great afternoon snack.

Serves 2

- ½ cup coconut milk (canned coconut milk gives a richer taste)
- 1 tablespoon blackstrap molasses or raw honey
- 1 tablespoon raw cacao powder (optional)
- 1-½ cups cooked quinoa
- ½-¾ cup Nut-Free Trail Mix (p. 81)

1) Pour coconut milk into saucepan placed over medium heat.

2) Add molasses or honey and cacao powder and stir until well mixed.

3) Add quinoa and stir until combined.

4) Stir in the trail mix. If consistency is too thick, add more coconut milk and serve up!

Rice & Egg Stir-Fry

This recipe is so adaptable. Sometimes I like to add a few baby greens and other leftover veggies that I've found in the fridge. If cooking for more than one, just double the recipe for every additional serving.

Serves 1

- 1 tablespoon coconut oil
- 1 cup cremini or white button mushrooms, thinly sliced
- ¼ cup diced green and red bell pepper
- ½ cup cooked rice
- 2 large eggs
- ¼ cup shredded cheddar Daiya or other cheese substitute
- Salt and pepper

1) Melt coconut oil in a medium skillet over medium-high heat.

2) Add mushrooms, peppers and rice, stirring constantly for approximately 2 minutes.

3) In a small bowl, beat the eggs.

4) Move rice and veggie mixture to one side of the skillet and pour eggs in same skillet, but on opposite side. Cook eggs, stirring around until they start to form solid pieces.

5) Stir veggies and rice into the eggs.

6) Remove from heat and sprinkle cheese substitute on top. Cover and set aside for a few minutes until cheese melts. Add salt and pepper to taste.

Quinoa Veggie Skillet

For a good start to your day, this breakfast dish is chockfull of protein and vitamins. The coconut aminos add extra flavor similar to adding soy sauce. Try scrambling in an egg for extra protein.

Serves 1

- 2 tablespoons coconut oil
- 2 cremini or other small mushrooms, diced
- ¼ cup coconut aminos
- ¼ teaspoon garlic powder
- 2 cups diced green and red bell peppers
- 1 cup cooked quinoa
- 1 cup mixed baby greens

1) Melt coconut oil in a large skillet over medium-high heat.

2) Sauté mushrooms 2-3 minutes.

3) Mix in coconut aminos and garlic powder.

4) Stir in peppers, quinoa and baby greens, mixing well until greens start to wilt. Serve immediately.

9) BREADS, SNACKS & DESSERTS

Coconut Flour Biscuits

These biscuits taste wonderful when they're slightly warm, topped with a little jelly or honey. They could also be served up as a bacon or sausage egg sandwich. If you're making bread instead of biscuits, cool the loaf completely before lifting it from the pan to help prevent cracking. For best results, all ingredients should be room temperature.

This recipe was adapted from and inspired by Leanne Vogel, Healthfulpursuit.com.[53]

Yield: 12 biscuits or 1 loaf

- 4 large eggs
- ⅔ cup full-fat canned coconut milk
- ¼ cup flax meal
- ¼ cup coconut oil
- 1 tablespoon apple cider vinegar
- 2 teaspoons raw honey
- 1 cup coconut flour, sifted
- ½ teaspoon baking soda
- ¾ teaspoon sea salt

1) Preheat oven to 350°F.

2) To make biscuits, line a baking sheet with parchment paper or a silicone baking sheet. Set aside. To make bread, oil a 9x13" loaf pan with coconut oil. Set aside.

3) Whisk the eggs on medium speed in the blender or using a standing mixer or hand mixer for 2 minutes until frothy.

4) Melt the coconut oil if it is solid at room temperature. Add coconut oil, apple cider vinegar and honey to the eggs and blend until well combined.

5) In a separate bowl, combine coconut flour, baking soda and salt.

6) Add dry flour mixture to the wet egg mixture and continue to mix on medium speed until combined.

7) To make biscuits, scoop the dough using a ¼ cup measure that has been greased with coconut oil for easy release of the dough, dropping the dough onto the baking sheet. To make bread, transfer dough to the prepared pan. Press down with the back of a spoon and smooth out.

8) Bake biscuits 25-30 minutes until tops are brown. Cool on a wire rack. Bake bread 45-50 minutes, until a toothpick inserted in the center comes out clean. Cool completely for at least 2 hours, then transfer to a cutting board to slice.

Grain-Free Sweet Potato Biscuits

These biscuits pair well with breakfast or dinner and have a natural sweetness to them from the potato without having to add any sweeteners to the ingredients. They also make a nutritious snack when your sweet tooth comes calling.

Yield: 6

- ¾ cup baked sweet potato, cooled completely with skin removed
- 3 large eggs
- 4 tablespoons coconut flour
- 1 teaspoon baking powder
- ¼ teaspoon salt
- 1 tablespoon chilled coconut oil

1) Preheat the oven to 350°F.

2) Beat the eggs with a whisk until well blended.

3) Add coconut flour, baking powder and salt and stir until a thick dough forms.

4) Mash the sweet potato, then combine it with the egg mixture.

5) Cut the coconut oil into the dough using a pastry cutter. This can also be done using two butter knives, holding one in each hand and cutting long strokes across the dough until the oil is incorporated. Dough will be very thick.

6) Line a baking sheet with parchment paper and use an ice cream scoop to form dough balls. Drop them onto the baking sheet, then use your hand to shape into biscuits.

7) Bake for 15 minutes or until golden brown.

Nut-Free Trail Mix

This recipe utilizes the ingredients that work best for my food sensitivities, but you can choose to add any dry ingredients you wish to personalize your trail mix. It's great to have on hand whenever you might need it.

This trail mix comes in handy when it's time to make muffins, Punkin' Chunkin' Cookie Bars (p. 82), Quinoa Porridge (p. 74), or Frosty Banana Pudding (p. 90), but I also like to eat it right from the bag as a snack when my sweet tooth comes calling!

- $\frac{1}{2}$ cup raisins
- $\frac{1}{2}$ cup sweetened dried cranberries
- $\frac{1}{2}$ cup dried blueberries
- $\frac{1}{2}$ cup dried pitted dates
- $\frac{1}{2}$ cup unsweetened coconut flakes
- $\frac{1}{2}$ cup raw unsalted pumpkin seeds
- $\frac{1}{2}$ cup raw unsalted sunflower seeds

Combine all ingredients in a resealable plastic bag, and shake. That's it!

Trail mix can be stored in the bag you made it in, or in a tightly sealed plastic container or jar.

Punkin' Chunkin' Cookie Bars

This recipe will make your house smell great while baking and the taste is so worth the effort of making them! This baked goodie doesn't make it to the cooling stage very often in my household.

Yield: 12-15 squares

- 1 cup Nut-Free Trail Mix (p. 81)
- ½ cup + 1 tablespoon coconut sugar
- 3 cups gluten-free all-purpose flour blend, or 1 cup each of sorghum, garbanzo bean and rice flour
- 1 teaspoon cinnamon
- 1 teaspoon baking soda
- ½ teaspoon salt
- ½ cup raw honey
- 2/3 cup coconut oil, melted
- 2/3 cup pumpkin puree
- 1 teaspoon pure vanilla extract
- ½ cup + 2 tablespoons old-fashioned oats[54]

1) Preheat oven to 350°F.

2) Line a 9x13" baking dish with parchment paper.

3) Pulse trail mix a few times in the food processor and set aside.

4) In a large bowl, combine ½ cup coconut sugar, flour(s), cinnamon, baking soda, and salt. Set aside.

5) In another bowl using an electric mixer, combine the honey, coconut oil, pumpkin and vanilla on medium speed.

6) With the mixer running, slowly add the dry ingredients to the wet. The batter will be very thick.

7) Add trail mix plus ½ cup of oats and stir to combine.

8) Spread batter into the prepared baking dish with your hands, wearing food-grade gloves or using a piece of plastic wrap to cut

down on the mess.

9) Sprinkle top with remaining 2 tablespoons of oatmeal.

10) Sprinkle remaining tablespoon of coconut sugar on top of the oatmeal and press down lightly.

11) Bake 25-30 minutes or until knife inserted in the center comes out clean and sides are pulling away. I like to bake mine a little longer to get crunchy edges.

12) Cool in the pan to lessen cracking, and then lift using the ends of the parchment as handles to move it to a cutting board. Cut into squares.

SB&J Plantain Roll-Ups

If you miss eating peanut butter and jelly sandwiches due to a grain and nut restriction, this substitute can help calm that craving. I prefer sunflower seed butter, or SB, but any type of seed or nut butter will work. The recipe calls for a thin layer of the butter and jelly to make for easier rolling, but I have a tendency to overload mine.

This recipe was adapted from and inspired by Simone Miller, Zenbelly.com.[55]

Yield: 10 roll-ups

- 3 large or 4 small yellow plantains, about 2-2.5 pounds before peeling
- 3 tablespoons coconut oil, melted
- 1/3 cup egg whites (about 2 large eggs worth)
- ½ teaspoon salt
- 1 teaspoon lime juice
- ¾ cup seed or nut butter of your choice
- ¾ cup jelly or fruit puree of your choice

1) Preheat oven to 350°F. Line a baking sheet with parchment paper and coat with coconut oil.

2) Peel and chop plantains to fit in food processor or blender.

3) Partially puree plantains, then add melted coconut oil, egg whites, salt and lime juice.

4) Drop by 2 rounded tablespoons per wrap onto a prepared baking sheet. Batter will be VERY thick and sticky. Spread out with the back of a spoon or with your fingers, getting the dough as thin as possible to approximately 5-6" in diameter, with about ½" between wraps. Wet fingers as needed to keep dough from sticking. Baking sheet should be able to hold 3-4.

5) Bake approximately 15 minutes or until dry to the touch with the edges just beginning to brown.

6) While still warm, spread the wraps with a thin layer of seed or nut butter and jelly, then roll up each one and move to a serving dish or lidded storage container. If you aren't going to be eating all of these roll-ups right away, they can be stored with parchment paper between layers to prevent sticking.

Storing the roll-ups without filling them with seed or nut butter and jelly first is also an option. Reheat in a warm oven or skillet before filling and rolling up to prevent cracking.

Coconut Whipped Topping

I like to use this coconut whipped topping as a frosting for cake. Other flavorings can be added, but I prefer to make it with just honey and vanilla. You can add 2-3 tablespoons of raw cacao powder and 3 tablespoons of raw honey to make it even sweeter. It can be used for a variety of recipes where a little creamy sweetness is desired. Try it as a substitute for dairy whipped topping on gelatin desserts, pumpkin pie and waffles, or as a coffee creamer. This recipe is a sure winner that can be adapted for many uses.

Keep in mind—coconut cream is not the same as coconut milk, since it has a higher fat content. If the recipe calls for cream (like this one does), it cannot be substituted.

- 2 13.5-ounce cans coconut cream, refrigerated overnight
- 1-2 tablespoons raw honey
- 1 teaspoon pure vanilla extract

1) Place a metal or glass bowl and mixer beaters in the freezer ahead of time, for at least 2 hours so they will be very cold.

2) Carefully open both cans of coconut cream. Scoop out the solid fat that has risen to the top and place in the chilled bowl. The liquid that's left in the can may be reserved for use in smoothies or other dishes.

3) Beat on high speed, adding the honey and vanilla gradually while the mixer is running. Beat ingredients for approximately 5 minutes or until stiff peaks form.

4) Refrigerate topping for 1-2 hours before serving or using to ice a cake, so it has a chance to firm up a little more.

Devil's Food Coconut Cake

My family loves, loves, loves this cake! The chocolatey goodness in every bite is complimented by the coconut whipped topping. Due to the quantity of moisture-absorbing coconut flour, this recipe requires a large amount of eggs that would be difficult to substitute.

This cake also bakes up nicely in a 9x13" pan. Just increase the baking time and check with a cake tester to be sure the cake has cooked through.

This recipe was adapted from and inspired by Lea Valle, Paleospirit.com.[56]

- ¾ cup melted coconut oil, plus more for greasing pans
- 1 cup coconut flour
- ¾ cup raw cacao powder
- ¾ teaspoon baking soda
- ¾ teaspoon sea salt
- 9 large eggs (Yes, you read that correctly)
- ½ cup pure maple syrup
- ½ cup raw honey
- ¾ cup brewed coffee or water
- 1-1/2 tablespoons pure vanilla extract
- 1 batch Coconut Whipped Topping (p. 87)
- ¼ cup raw, unsweetened coconut for topping the cake (optional)
- 1 teaspoon raw cacao powder (optional)

1) Preheat oven to 350° F.

2) Trace around two 9"cake pans onto parchment paper and cut out to form pan liners. Insert the liners and grease the sides and bottoms of the pans with coconut oil.

3) Combine coconut flour, cocoa powder, baking soda and salt in a small bowl and set aside.

4) Whisk the eggs in the bowl of a standing mixer fitted with the whisk attachment. Add the coconut oil, maple syrup, honey, coffee, and vanilla extract and continue to mix until combined.

5) Add the dry ingredients into the wet ingredients. Mix on low speed until fully incorporated, about 30 seconds. Scrape down sides of mixing bowl (you may need to do this a couple of times as you mix) and beat cake batter on high speed for about one full minute, until fluffy. The batter will be very thick.

6) Divide batter between the two pans, spreading it out evenly.

7) Bake for 30 minutes or until a toothpick inserted in the center comes out clean. Cake will not rise as high as if you were baking with traditional wheat flour.

8) Cool on a wire rack for 10-15 minutes. Use a knife to loosen the sides of the cake from the pan and turn out onto the wire rack. Cool completely.

9) After cake cools, place it in the fridge 1-2 hours to make it easier to apply icing.

10) Pull both cake pieces out of fridge, placing one on a cake plate.

11) Spread some of the coconut whipped topping on top of first layer, then place the second layer on top.

12) Begin icing on the sides and finish off with the top.

13) Sprinkle top with raw unsweetened coconut to your liking.

14) Sprinkle a fine dusting of cacao powder on top and it is ready to eat! Storing cake in the fridge will keep the icing nice and firm.

Frosty Banana Pudding

This delicious yet simple dessert is best consumed immediately. It does not keep its consistency well once frozen. However, if I have any left over, I will re-freeze in ice cube trays to mix into the occasional smoothie.

- 3 ripe bananas

  Additional optional ingredients:
- 1 tablespoon raw honey
- ½ cup Nut-Free Trail Mix (p. 81)
- 2 tablespoons raw cacao powder
- ¼ cup seed butter or nut butter of your choice
- ½ cup fresh or frozen strawberries or other fresh berries

  Use your imagination and add other tasty ingredients!

1) Dice bananas and place in freezer for two hours.

2) Once partially frozen, place slices in a high-speed blender or food processor and blend until creamy.

3) Blend in any optional ingredients.

Nut-Free Baked Apples

These apples have the best taste when served warm, and oh how fantastic your kitchen will smell! Serve as a dessert, snack, or even for breakfast.

- 1 tablespoon cinnamon
- ¼ cup raw pumpkin seeds
- ¼ cup raw sunflower seeds
- ¼ cup chopped and pitted dates
- ¼ cup raisins
- ¼ cup dried cranberries
- 6-8 apples (I like Gala)
- ½ cup ghee or coconut butter, divided
- ½ cup raw honey, divided

1) Preheat oven to 350°F.

2) Combine all ingredients except the apples, ghee or coconut butter and honey. I like to pulse in the blender for a couple seconds.

3) Melt ¼ cup of the ghee or coconut butter

4) Add melted ghee or coconut butter to ¼ cup of the honey and mix well. Combine with the dry ingredients and stir to coat well.

5) Remove cores from the apples and place in a 9x13" baking dish. Yes, I leave the peel on for the extra vitamins! Spoon filling into the center of each apple, filling to the top.

6) Combine the remaining melted ghee or coconut butter with the remaining honey and drizzle over the top of the apples.

7) Bake for 30 minutes. As the apples cook, they will release some liquid into the pan.

8) Once baked, spoon any liquid that's in the pan on top of the apples like a glaze and serve warm.

Cinnamon Stovetop Apples

In case you haven't noticed yet from the many recipes found in this book that contain cinnamon, my family just loves it! Warm apples go with any meal or as a stand-alone snack chockfull of vitamins.

- 6 apples (I like to use Fuji or Gala)
- ¼ cup water
- 1 tablespoon cinnamon
- 1 tablespoon raw honey or more to taste
- ½-¾ cup Nut-Free Trail Mix (p. 81) (optional)
- 1 tablespoon arrowroot powder or other thickening starch (optional)

1) Wash and cut the apples into chunks, leaving skins on (this is where that apple slicer gadget comes in handy!)

2) Place apples in a 2-quart saucepan with the water, cinnamon and honey over medium heat.

3) Cover and cook for 15-20 minutes.

4) Just before the apples are tender, add the trail mix and stir to combine.

5) Once the apples are tender and start falling apart, the juice should have the consistency of thick gravy. If too much liquid remains, combine arrowroot powder with 2 tablespoons of cold water in a small dish, stirring until dissolved completely. Stir the starch into the apples, cooking a couple extra minutes to thicken.

Flax & Oatmeal Raisin Cookies

I love oatmeal raisin cookies, but I was trying to incorporate a way to make them more nutritious, and easy to make using flax meal for an egg substitution. These babies are action packed with loads of fiber, and I think they taste better than standard oatmeal raisin cookies. They pair well with a cup of hot tea.

Yield: 2 dozen

- 5 tablespoons flax meal, divided
- 3 tablespoons warm water
- ½ cup all-purpose gluten-free flour
- 1-½ cups gluten-free oats
- ½ teaspoon cinnamon
- ¼ teaspoon chia seeds
- ½ teaspoon baking soda
- ½ teaspoon baking powder
- ¼ teaspoon sea salt
- ½ cup coconut oil
- ¾ cup coconut sugar
- 1 teaspoon pure vanilla extract
- ½ cup raisins (optional)
- ½ cup unsweetened coconut (optional)

1) In a small bowl, combine 1 tablespoon flax meal with the warm water. Mix well and set aside to thicken. This is a flax egg.

2) Preheat oven to 350°F and line 2 baking sheets with parchment paper.

3) Combine the flour, remaining flax meal, oats, cinnamon, chia seeds, baking soda, baking powder and salt in a medium bowl and set aside.

4) In another bowl using an electric mixer on medium speed, cream together the coconut oil and coconut sugar until well blended.

5) Add the vanilla and flax egg, and blend at low speed until well combined.

6) Add the dry ingredients gradually to the wet ingredients and continue to mix on low speed until well combined. The dough will be thick.

7) Add the raisins and coconut and continue to mix until well combined.

8) Using a small ice cream scoop, make balls and place on baking sheet an inch apart. Flatten out.

9) Bake 12-15 minutes or until golden brown, checking as the end of bake time approaches to make sure the cookies don't brown too much.

10) Remove from oven and cool cookies on baking sheet for 5 minutes before transferring to a cooling rack.

10) FURTHER READING

WEBSITES

The following are links to blogs and websites that I have found informative, many of which include helpful stories and tips related to living a healthy lifestyle.

Danielle Walker's Against All Grain	againstallgrain.com
Alison Needham's A Girl Defloured	agirldefloured.com
Amy Myers, MD	amymyers.com/myblog
Andrea Beaman, HHC, AADP, Chef	andreabeaman.com
Brian & Marianita Shilhavy's CoconutOil.com	coconutoil.com
Carrie Vitt's Deliciously Organic	deliciouslyorganic.net
Rick Davis's Eat Local Grown	eatlocallygrown.com
Gluten Free & More magazine	glutenfreeandmore.com
Gluten-Free Resource Directory	glutenfreeresourcedirectory.com
Gluten Free Society	glutenfreesociety.org
Nancy McEachern's Gluten Freeville	glutenfreeville.com
Green Living Hacks	greenlivinghacks.com

Healing the Body	healingthebody.ca
Leanne Vogel's Healthful Pursuit	healthfulpursuit.com
Michelle Toole's Healthy Holistic Living	healthy-holistic-living.com
Ali Maffucci's Inspiralized	inspiralized.com
Just Naturally Healthy	justnaturallyhealthy.com
Lexi's Clean Kitchen	lexiscleankitchen.com
Elizabeth Walling's The Nourished Life	livingthenourishedlife.com
Jason Wachob's Mind Body Green	mindbodygreen.com
Michelle Palin's My Gluten-Free Kitchen	mygluten-freekitchen.com
Lauren Goslin's Oatmeal with a Fork	oatmealwithafork.com
Kiersten Frase's Oh My Veggies	ohmyveggies.com
Organic Lifestyle magazine	organiclifestylemagazine.com
Paleo Living magazine	paleomagazine.com
Amy Green's Simply Sugar and Gluten-Free	simplysugarandglutenfree.com
Janie Bowthorpe's Stop the Thyroid Madness	stopthethyroidmadness.com
Steph Gaudreau's Stupid Easy Paleo	stupideasypaleo.com
Tiffany Pelkey's Coconut Mama	thecoconutmama.com
Sarah Ballantyne, PhD's The Paleo Mom	thepaleomom.com

BOOKS

The following are books from my own personal collection that I have read and found extremely helpful.

The Autoimmune Solution: Prevent and Reverse the Full Spectrum of Inflammatory Symptoms and Diseases by Amy Myers, M.D (2015)

Foods That Fight Pain: Revolutionary New Strategies for Maximum Pain Relief by Neal D. Barnard (1999)

Gluten-Free on a Shoestring, Quick and Easy: 100 Recipes for the Food You Love-- Fast! by Nicole Hunn (2011)

Hashimoto's Thyroiditis: Lifestyle Interventions for Finding and Treating the Root Cause by Izabella Wentz PharmD, FASCP (2013)

The Immune System Recovery Plan: A Doctor's 4-Step Program to Treat Autoimmune Disease by Susan Blum, M.D., M.P.H. (2013)

Living Gluten-Free For Dummies by Danna Korn (2010)

Nourishing Traditions: The Cookbook that Challenges Politically Correct Nutrition and the Diet Dictocrats by Sally Fallon (1995, 2001)

The Paleo Approach Cookbook: A Detailed Guide to Heal Your Body and Nourish Your Soul by Sarah Ballantyne, PhD (2014)

Simply Sugar and Gluten-Free: 180 Easy and Delicious Recipes You Can Make in 20 Minutes or Less by Amy Green (2011)

Winning the War Against Immune Disorders & Allergies by Ellen W. Cutler, D.C. (1998)

INDEX

cast iron, 39, 62, 67
cauliflower, 3, 5, 31, 36, 42, 45, 51, 53, 55, 65
celery, 33, 45, 47, 49, 51, 55, 67
celiac disease, 11, 12, 13, 14
cheddar, 53, 55, 73, 75
cheese, 44, 53
cheese substitute, 53, 55, 73, 75
chia seeds, 29, 92
chicken, 36, 47, 51
chicken broth, 37, 47, 51, 60, 66
chickpea, 14
chickpea flour, 14, 15
chili, 30, 31, 45, 47, 65
chili powder, 45
chocolate, 87
cinnamon, 70, 71, 72, 82, 90, 91, 92
clarified butter, 26
coconut, 15, 20, 26, 34, 81, 86, 87, 92
coconut aminos, 35, 51, 66, 76
coconut butter, 60, 90
coconut cream, 20, 72, 86
coconut flour, 3, 8, 15, 16, 72, 78, 80, 87
coconut milk, 19, 20, 28, 72, 74, 78, 86
coconut oil, 8, 25, 26
coconut palm sugar, 21
coconut sugar, 8, 21, 82, 92
coconut wraps, 33
coconuts, 3, 8
coffee, 87
coffee creamer, 86
cookies, 31, 32, 92
cooking fats, 24
cooking oils, 24
corn, 15, 29
corn oil, 24, 25
cornstarch, 15, 28, 51
cracker replacements, 32
crackers, 32, 33

cranberries, 81, 90
cream of tartar, 17
cremini mushrooms, 66, 75, 76
crepes, 32
cross-reactivity, 5
cruciferous, 5
cucumber, 33

D

dairy free, 44, 53
Daiya, 44, 53, 55, 73, 75
dates, 81, 90
dessert, 31
devil's food, 87
deviled eggs, 38
diet theory, 6
dried beans, 47
duck fat, 27

E

egg replacement, 30
egg sandwich, 78
egg substitute, 3, 28, 30, 92
eggs, 3, 15, 16, 27, 29, 30, 32, 35, 38, 73, 87
elimination diet, 14

F

fats, 24
flax meal, 3, 14, 15, 29, 31, 43, 49, 70, 71, 72, 78, 92
flax milk, 19
flaxseed, 14
flour blend, 15
food allergens, 5
french fries, 31
french toast, 38
frosting, 20, 86
frozen dessert, 89
fruit puree, 27, 30, 84

mustard, 63
mustard greens, 33

N

neutral flours, 15
nightshade, 5
noodles, 31, 36, 55
nutritional yeast, 42, 63
Nu-Wave Oven, 39, 53, 62

O

oat flour, 38
oats, 11, 38, 70, 82, 92
oils, 24
olive oil, 6, 8, 26
olives, 44
onion, 45, 47, 49, 51, 55, 57, 66, 67
oregano, 42, 47, 49, 63

P

paleo diet, 8, 15
pancakes, 31, 32, 38, 71
paprika, 62
parchment paper, 36
pasta, 31, 51, 55
pastries, 31, 32
peanut oil, 24, 25
pepper bacon, 61
peppers, 5, 44, 46, 49, 55, 75, 76
pesto, 31, 42
pie, 86
pizza, 42
pizza crust, 30, 31
plantain flour, 32
plantains, 32, 33, 84
polyunsaturated vegetable oils, 25
pork, 53
porridge, 74
potassium bitartrate, 17
potato skins, 53

potato starch, 15
potatoes, 30, 36, 53, 57, 60, 62
power flours, 14, 15
primal diet, 8
protein shakes, 31
psyllium, 29, 35
pudding, 89
pumpkin puree, 16, 27, 31, 37, 72
pumpkin seeds, 42, 81, 90

Q

quiche, 30
quinoa, 7, 8, 14, 36, 66, 74, 76
quinoa flour, 14

R

raisins, 81, 90, 92
rice, 3, 30, 36, 51, 65, 66, 75
rice flour, 11, 82
rice milk, 19, 28
rice wraps, 33
roast, 57
rye, 11

S

safflower oil, 24, 25
salad, 63
sauces, 38
sausage, 49, 73, 78
shortcuts, 35
shortening, 24
silken tofu, 30
slow cooker, 37, 39, 47, 49, 53, 57
smoothie, 89
sodium bicarbonate, 17
sorghum, 5, 14
sorghum flour, 15, 82
soup, 31, 38, 39
sour cream, 23
soy, 29

FOOTNOTES

[1] "Food Allergy." *AAAAI*. Web. 03 Feb. 2015. <http://www.aaaai.org/conditions-and-treatments/allergies/food-allergies.aspx>.

[2] "Mount Sinai study finds foods with baked milk may help build tolerance in children with dairy allergies." Mount Sinai Hospital. 30 June 2011. <http://www.mountsinai.org/about-us/newsroom/press-releases/mount-sinai-study-finds-foods-with-baked-milk-may-help-build-tolerance-in-children-with-dairy-allergies>.

[3] Ballentyne, Sarah. "The Whys Behind Autoimmune Protocol." *The Paleo Mom*. 10 Aug. 2012. Web. 03 Feb. 2015. <http://www.thepaleomom.com/2012/08/the-whys-behind-autoimmune-protocol.html>.

[4] Myers, Amy. "How to you're your gut healthy during the holidays." Dec. 2014. <http://www.amymyersmd.com/2014/12/how-to-keep-your-gut-healthy-during-the-holidays>.

[5] Lipman, Frank. "Digestive Disorders, Problems, Dysfunction & a Fix." 2015. <http://www.drfranklipman.com/digestion/>.

[6] Runyon, Joel. "Is Quinoa Paleo? A Deep Dive." 12 Dec. 2012. <http://ultimatepaleoguide.com/is-quinoa-paleo-a-deep-dive/>.

[7] Institute for Integrative Nutrition. <http://www.integrativenutrition.com/curriculum>.

[8] Avenin is the dominant prolamin recognized by the immune system of celiac patients, as demonstrated by detection of anti-avenin antibodies in their blood. Sjöberg, Veronika, et al. "Noncontaminated Dietary Oats May Hamper Normalization of the Intestinal Immune Status in Childhood Celiac Disease." *Clinical and Translational Gastroenterology*. 26 June 2014. <http://www.nature.com/ctg/journal/v5/n6/full/ctg20149a.html?WT.ec_id=CTG-201406>.

[9] FDA. "Questions and Answers: Gluten-Free Food Labeling Final Rule." 5 Aug. 2014. <http://www.fda.gov/Food/GuidanceRegulation/GuidanceDocumentsRegulatoryInformation/Allergens/ucm362880.htm>.

[10] Find more information here: Anderson, Jane. "Certified Gluten-Free Products." 10 Dec. 2014. <http://celiacdisease.about.com/od/glutenfreefoodshoppin1/a/ Certified-Gluten-Free-Products.htm>.

[11] Additional article on the effects of oats and a gluten-free diet can be found here: Osborne, Dr. "Certified Gluten Free Oats Prevent Recovery in Celiac Patients." *Gluten Free Society*. Web. 03 Feb. 2015. <http://www.glutenfreesociety.org/gluten-free-society-blog/certified-gluten-free-oats-prevent-recovery-in-celiac-patients/>.

[12] Follow this link to find Dr. Gourmet's comprehensive list of foods containing gluten. You may want to take this to the grocery store with you: http://www.drgourmet.com/gluten/pdf/containsgluten.pdf

[13] Gentile, Christina. "Celiac Disease and Mental Health." <http://www.celiaccentral.org/mental-health>.

[14] Wolfgang, David N. "Preventative Concerns On Neurological Aspects Of Celiac Disease Exposure To Heavy Metals In Relation To Alzheimer's Disease." 2013. <http://www.csaceliacs.org/alzheimers_disease_david_n_wolfgang.jsp>.

[15] The National Foundation of Celiac Awareness' Celiac Central website is a great resource for info on celiac as well as non-celiac gluten sensitivity. Visit http://www.celiaccentral.org/non-celiac-gluten-sensitivity/

[16] Visit Dr. Amy Myers' website at www.amymyersmd.com. She specializes in autoimmune disorders and discusses them in her blog.

[17] Hillson, Beth. "Power Flour: How to use Nutrient-Dense Flours in your Gluten-Free Baking." *Gluten Free & More.* Oct./Nov. 2011. Web. 03 Feb. 2015. <http://www.glutenfreeandmore.com/issues/4_16/power_flour-2653-1.html>.

[18] Jenny McGruther's blog gives more insight into the positives and negatives associated with using coconut flour. McGruther, Jenny. "How to Bake with Coconut Flour: Tips & Tricks for Using This Gluten-free Flour." *Nourished Kitchen.* 15 Dec. 2011. Web. 03 Feb. 2015. <http://nourishedkitchen.com/baking-with-coconut-flour/>.

[19] Helmenstine, Anne Marie. "What is the Difference Between Baking Soda & Baking Powder." 19 Feb. 2015. <http://chemistry.about.com/cs/foodchemistry/f/blbaking.htm>.

[20] This article is worth reading before you decide whether or not to use agave in your cooking. Mercola, Dr. "Agave Is Far Worse than High Fructose Corn Syrup." *Health Impact News.* 24 Oct. 2013. Web. 03 Feb. 2015. <http://healthimpactnews.com/2013/agave-is-far-worse-than-high-fructose-corn-syrup/>.

[21] "The Truth About Coconut Palm Sugar: The Other Side of the Story!" Web. 03 Feb. 2015. <http://www.tropicaltraditions.com/coconut_palm_sugar.htm>.

[22] Candida is a yeastlike fungus that lives inside the mouth and intestinal area. Its job is to aid digestion and nutrient absorption. An overgrowth of candida can break through the intestinal wall, invading the bloodstream and releasing toxins into the body. This causes leaky gut, which can lead to digestive disorders and other health problems. Myers, Amy. "10 Signs You Have Candida Overgrowth & What To Do About It." 4 April 2013. <http://www.mindbodygreen.com/0-8376/10-signs-you-have-candida-overgrowth-what-to-do-about-it.html>.

[23] For more stevioside comparison information, visit cookingwithstevia.com and emperorsherbologist.com/steviacompare.php.

[24] Gates, Donna and Ray Sahelian. "Stevia Conversion Chart." *The Stevia Cookbook* 1999. Reprinted and accessed via web. 03 Feb. 2015. <http://www.stevia.net/conversion.html>.

[25] "Blackstrap Molasses." Web 03 Feb. 2015. <http://www.med-health.net/Blackstrap-Molasses.html>.

[26] Machell, Laura. "How to Sweeten More Naturally." *The Green Forks.* 14 Feb. 2014. Web. 03 Feb. 2015. <http://thegreenforks.com/how-to-sweeten-more-naturally/>.

[27] Ibid.

[28] Fallon, Sally. *Nourishing Traditions* (2001).

[29] Ibid.

[30] Barron, Jon. "Fats and Oils Made Simple." *Healthy Fats & Oils: Natural Health Newsletter.* 07 Mar. 2011. Web. 03 Feb. 2015. <http://jonbarron.org/article/fats-and-oils-made-simple#.VJMsxf8kBg>.

[31] Fallon, Sally. *Nourishing Traditions* (2001).

[32] Ibid (see 30 and 31).

[33] For more information regarding the differences between clarified butter and ghee, as well as links to recipes for making both, visit: Davidson, Laura. "Butter 101: Clarified Butter, Ghee, and Brown Butter." *Blogging Over Thyme.* 16 October 2014. <http://www.bloggingoverthyme.com/2014/10/16/clarified-butter-ghee-and-brown-butter/>.

[34] Fallon, Sally. *Nourishing Traditions* (2001).

[35] "Egg Substitutes." *The Cooking Inn.* Web. 03 Feb. 2015. <http://www.thecookinginn.com/eggsub.html>.

[36] Angell, Brittany. "101 in Baking: Understanding Sugar, Butter, Eggs, Baking Soda & their Allergy Free Replacements." 24 May 2011. <http://brittanyangell.com/101-in-baking-understanding-sugar-butter-fats-eggs-baking-soda-their-allergy-free-replacements-in-baking/>.

[37] Bob's Red Mill Natural Foods, Inc. "Xanthan Gum or Guar Gum: Which Gum Should I Use?" *Bob's Red Mill.* <http://docs.bobsredmill.com/index2.php?option=com_docman&task=doc_view&gid= 5307&Itemid=29>.

[38] Ibid.

[39] Weingarten, Hemi. "10 Facts About Xanthan Gum, A Very Popular Food Additive." *Fooducate.* 23 Sept. 2010. <http://blog.fooducate.com/2010/09/23/10-facts-about-xantham-gum-a-very-popular-food-additive/>.

[40] Han, Emily. "Tofu Varieties: What's the Difference?" *The Kitchn.* 28 March 2014. <http://www.thekitchn.com/tofu-varieties-whats-the-difference-201345>.

[41] Bone, Kelly. "A Guide to Tofu Types and What to Do With Them." *Serious Eats.* 4 June 2014. <http://www.seriouseats.com/2014/06/shopping-cooking-guide-different-tofu-types.html>.

[42] To find out more about the nutritional properties of sweet potatoes, visit: http://whfoods.org/genpage.php? dbid=64&tname=foodspice.

[43] Avalon and Ryan. "Plantain Flour." *Culinary Adventures with Formschlag Jr.* 21 Nov. 2011. <http://cookingwithformschlagjr.tumblr.com/post/13149738622/plantain-flour>.

[44] Although I have not tried these yet, I'm intrigued by this recipe for plaintain slider buns from Steph Gaudreau at Stupid Easy Paleo. http://stupideasypaleo.com/2013/08/19/sweet-plantain-buns/

[45] Sarah Ballantyne gives step by step instructions for baking crackers with plantain flour on website, Paleo Mom. http://www.thepaleomom.com/2012/09/plantain-crackers-nut-free-egg-free.html

[46] Vogel, Leanne. "Coconut Biscuits." *Healthful Pursuit.* 16 Nov. 2014. Web. 03 Feb. 2015. <http://www.healthfulpursuit.com/2014/11/low-carb-coconut-flour-biscuits-bread/>.

[47] Vanilla powder is made from dried and ground pure vanilla beans, with no additives.

[48] Adapted from "Cooking Measurement Equivalents." *Infoplease.* Web. 03 Feb. 2015. <http://www.infoplease.com/ipa/A0001723.html>.

[49] For the USDA's take on cutting boards, visit: "Cutting Boards and Food Safety." 2 Aug. 2013. <http://www.fsis.usda.gov/wps/portal/fsis/topics/food-safety-education/get-answers/food-safety-fact-sheets/safe-food-handling/cutting-boards-and-food-safety>.

[50] Plan ahead and cook a big enough roast to have dinner tonight, plus leftover meat and potatoes for the next night's meal!

[51] From episode 7 of the first season of *Happy Days*.

[52] If using a large muffin tin, add two additional eggs. Egg substitutes are not recommended for this recipe.

[53] Vogel, Leanne. "Coconut Biscuits." *Healthful Pursuit.* 16 Nov. 2014. Web. 03 Feb. 2015. <http://www.healthfulpursuit.com/2014/11/low-carb-coconut-flour-biscuits-bread/>.

[54] Quick-cooking oats will also work, but I prefer using old-fashioned oats for this recipe.

[55] Miller, Simone. "Plantain Tortillas." *Zenbelly.* 17 Aug. 2013. Web. 03 Feb. 2015. <http://zenbellycatering.com/2013/08/17/plantain-tortillas/>.

[56] Valle, Lea. "Paleo Chocolate Birthday Cake." *Paleo Spirit.* 30 June 2012. Web. 03 Feb. 2015. <http://paleospirit.com/2012/paleo-chocolate-birthday-cake-coconut-honey-frosting/>.

Made in the USA
San Bernardino, CA
29 November 2018